# WE ARE
# UNBREAKABLE

## Raw, Real Stories of Resilience
### FROM WOMEN IN NOVA SCOTIA IN 2020

# KAREN DEAN

For further information, please address:
hello@KarenDeanSpeaks.com

Cover and book design by Rebecca Wilson of Offshoot Creative Consulting.

———

For all of the incredible souls
who were taken from us
so tragically in 2020,
but especially to my friend,
and a friend to many,
the fierce, kind, and beautiful,
Gina Goulet

Gina,
I miss your smile, your laugh
and your kickass attitude.
But I feel your spirit every day and
I thank you for pushing me to do more
and to help others more than ever before.
The voice in my head that pushes me forward
will forever be named Gina.

*Man, it ain't right, man it ain't fair*
*I'll see you again, but till then*
*Give heaven some hell*
*— Hardy*

XOXO
Karen

# Table of Contents

# FOREWORD

The Nova Scotia Remembers Legacy Society evolved out of a desire to do something when we all felt so helpless in the face of the unspeakable loss we experienced in rural Nova Scotia as the result of the shooting in April 2020 in which 23 lives were taken from their families and communities. On that Sunday morning in April, and in the days that followed, rural Nova Scotia longed for the opportunity to share with each other in our grief, but with the Covid-19 lockdowns firmly in place, we could not do that in person in the way that we needed to, to hold each other in our shock and pain. As a result, community members, through the magic of social media and some great friends came together to develop and create the online vigil, Nova Scotia Remembers, that was broadcast across Canada on April 24th as a tribute to those lost, their families, and the communities at the centre of this tragedy.

From this tribute, arose the desire to create a legacy, one that shines the brightest light into the darkness we were left with following those first difficult days. The vision of this legacy is one that will, over the long run, lift up those experiencing the deepest loss and the communities whose resilience will be their pillar of strength moving forward. Our society will seek to achieve this vision by supporting education, grief and trauma supports, and community development initiatives. Further, we will work directly with families, communities, governments, and other stakeholders in establishing and maintaining, one or more permanent long-term memorials to ensure we always remember those who were so unfairly taken from us.

I want to take the time to thank you for your support of our work through the purchase of this wonderful book that showcases 22 beautiful Nova Scotian women who define resiliency and strength in 2020. The proceeds of this work will establish a bursary program aimed at women in our communities who have overcome adversity and barriers to pursue their education and that demonstrate those qualities of resiliency and strength that are captured here in these pages.

Please join us in our journey by visiting our webpage at www.novascotiaremembers.ca or find us on Facebook.

Much love <3

Tiffiany Ward
   *Chair*
   *Nova Scotia Remembers Legacy Society*

# INTRODUCTION

2020 is a year that will go down in worldwide history as the year of the global pandemic. But here in Nova Scotia, we will mostly remember it as a year of tragic loss and heartache.

While we were dealing with the Covid-19 restrictions and a provincial State of Emergency that lasted almost all year, we had one tragedy after another, after another. There was a horrific mass shooting that took the lives of 22 innocent victims and one unborn baby. There was a helicopter crash off of the coast of Greece that took the lives of military personnel based in Nova Scotia. Then one of the Snowbirds Air Demonstration aircraft crashed in British Columbia and took the life of another Nova Scotian. A 3-year old boy went missing in Truro, Nova Scotia. It seemed like the bad news just kept coming and the people of Nova Scotia could not catch a break.

But, through it all, the incredible people of Nova Scotia came together and showed strength like I have never seen. We supported our neighbours. We boosted our communities. And we showed our pride in our beautiful little province.

This inspirational book is a collection of stories written by a group of phenomenal women who call Nova Scotia home. I asked some of the most amazing women I know to share their experience of the unprecedented year of 2020. These women come from many walks of life and age groups. You will see from their stories that we have all had different challenges and experiences this year.

However, we have all had one thing in common: our resilience.

I hope the words on the following pages bring you some inspiration, some comfort through difficult times, and some connection to the women who have so graciously shared their stories.

We will always remember those who we lost and feel their spirits as they watch over and guide us.

We will see them in the incredible Nova Scotia sunsets.

We will hear them when the winds blow.

We will honour them with our stories and build a legacy to make them proud.

Much love to you all,

Karen Dean

Take care
and be kind,
Karen

# Amy Hill

2019 was a rough one, both physically and mentally. It actually started with the biggest high of my life – birthing my son into my husband's hands in our kitchen with only the calm of our home and my beautiful birth worker and friend, Jessica, surrounding us. It was an experience that would help to push me through a year filled with more work than we should have taken on with a newborn in tow including the attendance of new markets, expanding our garden spaces and greenhouse production, taking on secondary processing of our meat products at an inspected kitchen, and increasing our ability to sell to retail markets. By the end of the year I had a cranky, clingy baby who didn't sleep, a back that felt broken from wearing him all day, a 6-year-old who wanted more family time, a body and mind that had worn thin from almost ten years of business building – I needed a break. And 2020 looked like the break I needed. We sat down with our accountant in early January and mapped out our projections; it was going to be the year we finally turned a profit. We had all of the right things in place. We wrote it on our big calendar – THIS IS GOING TO BE OUR YEAR!

And then it wasn't... or at least, it wasn't anything that resembled the year we thought it would be.

My husband, David, and I run our mixed farming operation, Snowy River Farms, on 9.97 acres in Cooks Brook, Nova Scotia. We started our farm from scratch back in 2011 and purchased our current property in the Fall of 2012 where we began to build it from the ground up. I imagine taking over a farm from family members is not an easy task under even the best of circumstances, but I can attest to the difficulties you face when starting one on bare land with no livestock base, buildings, gardens or customers to slide into. We have spent the last almost ten years putting every penny earned (and then some) back into our farm in order to grow it into the business we have today which is large enough to provide work for both me and David full time, year-round. Until 2017 Snowy River was run entirely by myself (and our daughter that we welcomed in 2013) while David worked off farm to cover expenses, so having him home the past three years has meant extra hands available which is so, so good, but also a great increase in work load in order to pull in enough financially to keep us both working here.

I promised myself at the beginning of 2020 that I was going to make my mental health, my physical health, and my emotional health a priority. I booked in 6 months worth of chiropractic care to improve the physical, we were lining up an Au Pair to watch the kids so that I could mentally tackle the areas of the farm that I run without the distractions that come with children under your care, and we had said we would take a week long family vacation after the growing season, which was pretty big for us as we typically get away for maybe three weekends a year if we're lucky and hadn't been outside of the Atlantic Region since our honeymoon back in 2012. We were so pumped for the year. But then March came.

We have always had this idea here that we are safe, provided for. That we don't work for anyone but ourselves which means we have work as long as we want to have work. We create our own customer base, we can increase or decrease product availability based on the markets – essentially, we have felt like the world could crash and we would still be ok here because people always need to eat and, at the very least, we can provide all of the food we need. We were incredibly blind to weaknesses that our business had and they were about to have a great big spotlight shined on them.

Covid-19 started with an extension of our daughter's March Break by a couple of weeks. Within a few days the lock downs began to trickle in, day by day more restrictions were put in place and with every restriction came another barrier to our ability to sell products. In one day we had every restaurant and store that sold our products call to cancel their weekly deliveries. Our Farmer's Markets stayed open for a couple of weeks, trying to funnel customers through to keep with social distancing require-ments but that ended as well as they closed their doors, unable to meet regulations. Our Au Pair that we had been speaking with wouldn't be able to come into the Country as borders closed. Volunteers known as WWOOFers that we take in each year for help couldn't come into Canada. Everyone was told not to interact with those outside of their household – so we lost all avenues for childcare. The inspected kitchen we were using to make our sausages closed. We couldn't get anyone in to help finish the poultry barn we were building. We couldn't hire for the planting season. We were terrified. The government released biweekly payments for those who were out of work due to Covid but we didn't qualify as business owners. They released funding for entrepreneurs but we again didn't qualify because we had not collected an income from our farm as all funds leading up to this year went back into building greenhouses, pastures and poultry barns. We seemed to fall through every crack there was and we suddenly had no idea how we were going to pay our mortgage or phone and electricity bills. The meat in the freezers and vegetables in the gardens wouldn't sustain us if we couldn't afford to keep our property.

I remember sitting in the living room with David one afternoon stewing in this feeling of panic and unsure what to do. We had lost all of the avenues to make money that we had thought were ours and were safe. Was this year that was supposed to showcase all that we had been working towards, the year that we finally started being rewarded for our efforts, actually going to be the year that we closed our doors? I felt like we were trapped in this avalanche of work that needed to be done without being able to hire help and no sales to cover our operational costs. It was the scariest and most heartbreaking time our business had ever faced and we were so worried that we were about to lose it all. Our minds were racing and through our panic we just started listing off ways we could possibly stay open – and we found one.

I could create an online store and inventory all of the product we had on hand, updating the available greens, eggs and vegetables weekly, accepting payments online and delivering items direct to our consumers without coming in contact with them. It would mean a complete website overhaul during a time when libraries were closed and our rural internet was less than cooperative, but it looked like it was our only shot at getting our product to our customers reliably. Within a week I had updated our whole website including a page where all orders could be processed and, with many, many glitches along the way, I could also have customers sign up for weekly farm boxes through our CSA (Community Supported Agriculture) and select their pick up or delivery locations.

Covid hit us at the worst possible time of the year. March is when the majority of our transplants are started. In April we are able to start harvesting food from the greenhouses and are busy potting up lots of plants as well as starting our meat birds for the year. May sees us full time in the gardens and greenhouses planting, weeding and harvesting. What we are able to set up in the Spring affects how we will be able to pay our bills for the rest of the year. If we are unproductive from February to June we won't have enough plants in the ground to harvest for the season. It affects at least 75% of our income. I couldn't lean on friends to watch our kids because we weren't supposed to be in contact with anyone else and we were struggling to figure out how to hire during a pandemic. It was sun up to sun down work in either the fields or barns or online tweaking website issues while Fridays were spent driving orders to customers. April also saw the largest mass shooting in Canada's history take place literally minutes from where we live and seeing how many people around us were directly affected weighed heavily on our hearts, and all Nova Scotians collectively. It was a time when we were all mourning but without having the ability to release with friends and family the way we all needed. The workload during that time felt heavier than I had ever experienced and I wasn't really sure how we were going to be able to keep up that pace.

We ended up doing our own deliveries in the beginning but after two months of driving for 12+ hours each Friday with the kids in the car we decided to hire out that job. Those drives were a really important step in realizing what areas we were needed in and which ones we could safely hire for. We had long discussions about what was working for us and which areas we really needed to change because they were too draining. During this time we also found an Au Pair in Canada who could come and live with us since daycares had only opened at half capacity and were not taking in any new kids. We knew that at this point, while we are a very healthy household and did not personally fear getting this virus, our business would not survive a 14-day shut down if we did come into contact with someone who tested positive. So, there was this dance we were having with needing more help but not wanting to bring in too many people and risk being put into isolation because of it. We decided though, that the work load ahead was far too great to tackle alone. Our Au Pair ended up bringing her partner with her to work alongside us for a month

5

and we hired two more full time employees, along with a weekly volunteer and spent the rest of the summer with our heads down, tackling the driest June and July we have ever seen along with insanely high temperatures and pushed for online sales in every avenue we could find. A couple of the stores that had previously carried our products had created their own online space with contactless delivery or curb-side pick-up as well and were beginning to accept our goods again. Farmer's Markets also developed an online pick-up option and we slowly started figuring out how to track inventory over multiple locations so that we could keep sales moving and have our product as accessible as possible.

If I'm being honest, much of the summer is a blur. We were finishing projects in August that were supposed to be done back in March. Every week was spent trying to get our veggie boxes planned for and harvested while putting in irrigation or new greenhouses that were behind because of hold ups from Covid. We rarely had a day to ourselves where we didn't discuss how we were going to try and move sales to new areas in order to cover costs. It felt like a marathon without an ending and, with so many of our sales moving from retail at markets to wholesale through new stores, we were seeing less money coming in for more product moving out. September 21 brought in a kill frost. Temperatures dipped low enough to kill off our cucumbers, sweet peppers, tomatoes, melons, zucchini and squash. It was incredibly frustrating as I knew the temperatures for the next month would all be perfect for growing but it was also a much-needed reason to stop and regroup. I knew that we needed to find some time to actually step back and look over our entire operation. We needed to be able to set ourselves up for this "New Normal" that could last another month, year, maybe forever. And we needed to be stopped by something bigger because without that we would honestly just keep going with our heads down.

I work every year with a group who helps youth facing barriers to the work force gain skills needed to build their resumes and find meaningful employment. This Fall we took on 8 amazing humans who, instead of helping us plant more produce in all available spaces of the gardens as we typically would, helped us to close up beds, build new greenhouse structures for 2021 growth, and really just prepare ourselves for whatever next season wants to give us. With their extra hands I've been able to sit down and take in all the lessons we learned this year – what brings us joy, what isn't worth our time, what helps us to be better farmers, friends and soil builders, and what we need to do to make sure that we are meeting our end goal of creating a space that is healthy for our land, our livestock and ourselves. We spent much of this year with our heads down, just working until it is over as if at midnight on January 1, 2021 it will all magically reset itself.

I realized recently that the chaos stops when we make it stop. Nothing will change for next year if we don't back up and apply the things we have learned through this year. That it doesn't happen on January 1st, it happens whenever we want it to happen. Covid-19 was a huge hit financially, mentally, and physically but I'm sure if it hadn't been a Global Pandemic there would have been something else that would have worked its way in to keep us busy and, while I don't wish to live this year all over again, I certainly learned a lot and became far more organized than I could have ever imagined. There are many procedures that we have put in place that will continue well past this virus and I will be forever grateful for the push that was given (however harsh and scary it felt at the time) to create our online store as that will benefit us well into the future. I don't want to look back at this year as the worst year of our lives. I want to look back at it as the year I learned the most and saw what we are capable of under the most extraordinary of circumstances. I want to see how amazing our friends and family were when they saw us struggling and could find creative ways to help. I want to remember our customers who supported us through all of the changes. We'll come out stronger not in spite of it all, but rather because of it.

---

## About Amy Hill

Amy Hill was raised in the city with a heart for country living and finally brought her sustainable living dreams to life in 2011 when she started a farm with her (now) husband, David. Together they tend to mixed livestock and a market garden on their small acreage in Cooks Brook, NS alongside their daughter, Ayla (7) and son, Ezekiel (2). They raise pigs and chickens on fruits and vegetables, certified nonGEO grains, and rotated pastures and grow a large variety of spray-free, heirloom vegetables for sale at both Farm Markets, local produce stores and from their own property. Through social media she shares the ups and down of agriculture and tries her best to educate consumers on food production and how to create beautiful, healthy meals with locally sourced products.

http://www.snowyriverfarms.com/
IG and FB: @snowyriverfarms

# Amy VanderHeide

HARD-WORKING • PASSIONATE • LOYAL • WILLING TO LEARN • HUMBLE

Easter Weekend was the first time I cried.

I'm a farmer. I farm with my husband and my in-laws in the Annapolis Valley, beautiful no matter what time of year and a place where it is easy to imagine that you're far away from the rest of the world.

Early in March 2020, I travelled to PEI for a Young Farmer conference. Aside from the excitement of meeting other farmers from across the country, there was a noticeable undertone through-out the weekend. Increasing numbers of hand hygiene stations were scattered throughout and everyone seemed to be asking "have you heard about that weird virus going around?"

The next week, after arriving home and preparing for March Break with 3 kids it became clear that Canada was now under siege. Very quickly, we started to wonder – would school start back up? Should we keep our children home for a while longer? That week seemed to last forever, all the 'what ifs, hows and whys' that went through my mind seemed never ending. The insomnia that hits me whenever things get stressful hit like a freight train.

Did I mention that my father-in-law is in his 70s with a history of heart disease and my husband has Multiple Sclerosis (MS)? On top of wondering what we'd do if school was cancelled, we were now hearing stories of the many deaths and severe cases along with how important it was going to be to protect those at high risk.

The unknown is always the scariest, so when we learned that schools would be closed it took some of the worry away. Although we weren't sure how long the schools would be closed, I was fairly certain that no matter what, my children would be staying home. We had to protect those close to us first and foremost.

The fear was dissipating knowing we could keep our distance from others easily, as we don't leave the farm that often anyhow. However, a new stress was creeping in – How was I supposed to work full-time on the farm during our busiest time of the year with 3 kids home from school and no daycare option? Aside from the busyness of planting season, haying season, barn rotations and the normal day to day chores, we'd also been preparing for a major barn renovation. As with most of our renovation/building jobs, we'd been planning to do the majority of the work ourselves. How would I cope knowing my husband and father-in-law would be pulling double-duty as they filled in the gap left by myself, and a student that was not returning this year? (Luckily, he did come back! Due to COVID-19, he wasn't able to take the job he'd hoped to fulfill this summer so we had an extra set of experienced hands to help get us through the most laborious tasks.) We always have a summer childcare plan, however we didn't plan on March Break being the beginning of summer vacation.

Farming is not an easy job, its not always a safe job and we don't have set hours. None of those things are conducive to having 2 elementary school children along for the ride every day. Our oldest son is 12 and has become a great help on the farm. As much as I dislike how fast our kids seem to be growing up, I was so happy that at least one of them was old enough to be of help and also be somewhat independent if we needed him to be.

All of those thoughts, worries and stresses played on a continuous loop for weeks. We managed the day by day, and although it was different for us to be home together that time of year, we made the most of it and were happy that we were able to be together and have the space we have to roam and play.

Despite all of that happening in my head, dragging me down and exhausting me mentally and physically, it wasn't until Easter Dinner arrived, homecooked and hand delivered by my grandparents. To the doorstep. That it really hit me. They left the food by the door, gave a quick honk so we knew they were there, and they drove off to do the same deliveries to my parents and my brother's houses. We dished out our family meal for the kids, sat down and ate together. And then I cried.

It's funny how you can go through so much and deal moment-by-moment and then reality hits you like a hurricane. I wasn't sad about school or about work. I wasn't worried about how we'd keep up with all of our summer jobs. I missed my family. I missed the hug from my grandmother, the peck on the cheek from my grandfather. I missed hearing my brother, who always has something funny to tell us about something that happened on a job site, or my nephew, who may be a bit like his father, and always has a big story to tell. I missed my dad mashing the potatoes and showing off the turkey he fried, and my mom's grin when I catch her saying something under her breath when she thinks no one is listening. Nothing else mattered at that moment but my family, all who live within 20 minutes of me, but whom I hadn't been able to physically touch for over a month. I'll never take a hug for granted again.

The next week that longing for family was heightened even

11

more when the unspeakable tragedy that occurred in our province touched everyone in one way or another. I didn't know any of the victims personally, but it seems we all know someone who knew someone. It is safe to say that everyone will remember that day above all as the darkest day, pandemic or not, in our province's history. Nova Scotia will grieve that day for many years to come.

Truth be told, the next few weeks after that weekend in April seemed to be gone for me. I remember turning the TV on being exhausting. I couldn't bear to hear or see any more headlines about loss or devastation and in those moments, I'm not sure exactly what we did during that time, but I remember feeling thankful for our health and each other and that's what we focused on.

As Spring set in the work on the farm started coming on faster and we found ourselves in a bit of a lurch regarding how we would manage on the farm without any of the kids in daycare. In the past, we used part-time daycare and relied on my mother-in-law's help on the days that the kids were home. We also took advantage of Bible School and other day camps, as well as a week away at an overnight camp. Between those options, although it was still chaotic, we knew that the kids had a schedule and most importantly, I was able to be on the farm and know that my kids were safe and being taken care of. I thrive when I am working. I'm a much better mother to them when I can also work and a better person to be around altogether. I loved staying home with them when they were babies but once they were old enough to start nursery school and school I was very much ready to be working again. So, knowing the amount of work that needed to be done, how laborious that work is, I felt so guilty at the thought that I wouldn't be able to contribute. No daycare, no camps, and my mother-in-law had hopes of stepping back from childcare. We also wanted to protect her and my father-in-law as health officials continually advised watching out for those most vulnerable.

Mostly, I was sad. I felt like I was being pushed backwards. I've worked so hard to be able to work full-time on the farm. I've paid for it with my own dirt, sweat and tears. As a woman in agriculture, I felt like I was being forced back into a role I didn't feel like I fit into anymore. I struggled thinking about spending the entire summer feeling like that. I couldn't sleep, I couldn't focus, and I just wanted this all to be over. Knowing that wasn't possible, I decided that asking around to see how others were managing this particular hurdle could be helpful.

Part of my daily life includes being a Co-Creator of the Maritime Ag Women's Network (MAWN) along with one of my favourite women in agriculture, and best friend, Katie Keddy. We started this network 5 years ago to build a small community of women who worked and lived similarly to how we do, and so we could all reach out and be there to support each other. Through-out the Spring, many members were posting questions about how other farms and families were meeting the challenges the pandemic was throwing at us. Once we posted about childcare, the page blew up with replies. So many of us were in the same predicament and unsure what we could do. Some were hoping they could hire summer students, some were trying to find out if they could use grants and funds designated for summer students to put towards in-home childcare. Nothing worked. There was no help for this issue. It was on us. Unprepared financially, many of us had to make major changes in our day-to-day to make things work for our children. It is what parents do everyday, but when you are the sole caretaker for your business and your children, you make extra sacrifices. Your bread and butter, your future, your children's future, all stems from one place. It is a lot to carry. I, along with Katie, and MAWN member Amy Hill, banded together to tackle childcare. Going into a busy summer, it seemed we were each pulled away for interviews every week or so. We sent letters, so many letters to the Premier, to our MLAs, our MPs, to anyone who we thought would listen. After a solid effort with help from the Federation of Agriculture, we hit a wall. There was no help. We were on our own.

During this time of joining together with this group of fierce women, I was looking to anyone who had suggestions regarding how I could find someone to help with childcare. Luckily, I have a friend, who is an Early Childhood Educator at a local community college daycare, who helped me with figuring out wages and writing an ad to put out through the college and anywhere else I could think of to find help. She also suggested I contact her neighbour, who was a student at a local high school, with hopes of going in to Early Childhood Education after graduation in 2021. In perhaps our luckiest moment of the whole pandemic, she called me and immediately accepted our terms. With that, we had a 9-5, 5 days a week babysitter. I really think she was a gift to us, my kids loved her after the first day, she fit in with us so well and she saved my sanity. We are now 2 months into the school year and I'm still paying off debt from summer childcare expenses, and I can say with complete happiness that it was worth it. However, childcare support programs that allow people to hire students for childcare need to be implemented. A national childcare strategy would be incredibly welcome, and I have hopes that going through this pandemic, or the "she" session as it has been referred to, has opened many eyes to the issues still affecting women in the workplace. Looking into next year, or the next wave, whatever happens next, I hope that, above all, we see vast improvements in specific areas to support women and children.

With childcare covered for the summer, I felt much better. I was able to work, be a good mom, and have time with my family to enjoy the summer in the Annapolis Valley. We spent time in the water visiting the lakes and shores. Explored our backyard more than ever. We were thankful by Father's Day that we were able to have a small family gathering and hug our parents and grandparents. Those first hugs are etched in my heart and that family time has never been more cherished. Summer birthdays and holidays were spent enjoying each other and soaking in all of that time. Now that we know how quickly it can all be taken away, we learned to appreciate it all so much more.

In the middle of all of this, my husband underwent a

second treatment for his MS. This treatment required travelling to Halifax from the Annapolis Valley each day for 3 days of IV infusion. While we normally wouldn't bat an eye at the travel, with everything else going on, it seemed like a huge task. We'd have to think about where we should stop if we needed to, how to plan meals and snacks because I wouldn't be able to leave the infusion treatment once we were in for the day. Last year, during his first round, I would leave during the day to shop or pick up our lunches. The first round was 5 days and those escapes help break up the time before the drive back home at the end of the day. Our biggest fear, of course, was the unknown of if the treatment would put him at more risk of contracting COVID-19, and if it did, how hard it would be on him if he were to catch it. His neurologist was very reassuring, and as his treatment had already been delayed by a few months, he felt it was very safe at the time for him to have his treatment and stay low risk of coming into contact with any cases. We were also concerned about the months ahead, as his infusions essentially killed off his immune system for a few months. His doctor explained to us that although the thought of COVID-19 was daunting, he would be at more risk of catching the flu or a cold. Of course, the scariest would be if he were to contract influenza and then come into contact with COVID-19. As all of that was hypothetical, and he would be set back even farther and have to start all over again if we waited too long, we went ahead with it and he finished up his treatment with no issues, aside from a few headaches and fatigue. Now that we are here with flu season upon us, the concern is still there in the back of my mind but, at the end of the day, we know we have done everything we can to protect him. We have all had our flu shots, we all follow public health protocols and as we always do, we keep an eye on anything that may interfere with his health. Health is always a priority.

Sitting here now, a few weeks after Thanksgiving, spent with great food and a lot of love, I feel somewhat melancholic. We know a second wave is now sweeping across the country and we're likely just at the beginning of it. We've been so lucky to have the protection of the Atlantic Bubble for this long and we can only hope it holds strong. However, its like there is something behind me, making the hair on the back of my neck prickle every now and then. A reminder that we are not yet out of the woods. Yet at the same time, a reminder that we got through it once and the resilience learned, resilience earned really, from those experiences will make me stronger and more prepared for whatever comes at us next.

## About Amy VanderHeide

Amy calls the beautiful and diverse landscape of the Annapolis Valley, Nova Scotia home. She grew up next door to her grandmother's beef farm and now farms full time with her husband and in-laws on their poultry and crop farm. She and her husband also own a small beef herd on the side. She and her husband James have 3 sons, ages 6, 8, and 12, who can usually be found tagging along with either one of their parents on the farm.

In 2015, she and Katie Keddy founded the Maritime Ag Women's Network, which connects women in all areas of agriculture and farming throughout the Maritimes.

Amy is highly active in her community, as a 4-H leader, a director on several agriculture and non-agriculture boards. She's passionate about farming, food and working with youth.

# ANGELA MERCER-PENNY

## Thank You For That

Dear Universe,

Girl...I know you said you had my back, but can we talk about your methods for a minute?

What the heck was up with the entire 2020 year?

Remember in January how I was sooo pumped to launch an entire line of makeup to go with my skincare? Did you truly understand my disappointment with being unable to source my supplies? By February I became hyper aware of exactly where my packaging and ingredients were coming from when everything came to a complete standstill on the other side of the world. I've always been proud to order Canadian, and it forced me to really take inventory of where my Canadian suppliers were actually sourcing products. When nothing was coming from China it really hit us in the manufacturing industry hard.

So, locally made didn't always mean locally sourced components, and I had such an epiphany and vowed to do better.

So thank you for that.

And hey Girl, remember how for the 13 years that my husband travelled for work I was here as a solo parent managing everything by myself, the kids, the home, the businesses, the farm, the stress? Remember how I'd cry at every single airport drop off and beg for a way to all live together under one roof?

You sure do have a sense of humour, don't you?

In my controlling nature I sort of envisioned a plan that involved a transition of sorts. You know, like with work, with conversations, with a strategy.

I did not expect to pick my husband up on that Thursday afternoon and by the weekend everything came to a screeching halt. No job. No air travel. No plan.

And I know I asked to live with him, but still do other things. Like leave the house.

Instead though, we had to figure out if we even liked each other. Forced into lockdown together after 13 years of being two independent souls who talked everyday and saw each other for a few days a month but didn't even know how to actually live together.

When did I get so picky about how the bed was made?

Did he always snore this loud?

How did we become the couple whose favorite pastime was seeing which birds came to the feeder?

I mean we're grandparents, but cool ones, aren't we? No. I guess we're the "Don't forget more birdseed when you go to the store" kind of cool.

But you know what? I like him. And he likes me. And after a bit of adjustment and a new job here at home, we are all living together under one roof.

So, thank you for that.

And Girl, remember how I had so many tough things to process and I just used to keep myself really really busy instead of facing some hard truths?

When there's not much to do, and nowhere to go, and no people stopping by, it kind of makes it hard to avoid stuff for long, doesn't it?

I took a big long hard look at my patterns, my beliefs, my intuitive gifts, my inner child, and I finally did the work that I'd always been too scared to face. It was hard, it was messy, but it was work that I had to do and the only way I was ever going to do it was to take away all of the busyness that I ran towards. It took halting the world to heal myself from the inside out.

So, thank you for that.

And Universe, I've found more gratitude in connections, and hugs, and family and health. I've deepened my faith, I've loosened the reins on trying to control everything, and I've traded chaos for peace.

So thank you for that.

Girl, I know you always have my back, I'll trust that wholeheartedly now.

Thank you for that.

## About Angela Mercer-Penny

Angela Mercer-Penny is a small-town big dreamer, with a soft spot for animals and witchy intuitive gifts that make her super fun at parties. She owns Grit and Grace Skincare and lives in Cape Breton with her husband and is the proud Mother of three children and Lolli to one granddaughter.

# CARLEY GLOADE

EMPOWERED • CAPABLE • FEISTY • THOUGHTFUL • LEADER

My year began like everyone else for the most part, my spouse returned home from a successful fishing season and we rang in the New Year with family. We were planning our annual trip to Jamaica and enjoying the life we have worked hard to build. Looking back, it was a quiet evening considering what we were about to endure.

In January 2020, I decided to run for a spot in Chief and Council. For anyone that knows me, I wear my heart on my sleeve and nothing that comes out of my mouth is filtered or sugar coated. So, let's just say I wasn't sure how well I would fare in an election. I got to work on my campaign, I posted signs from here to goodness knows where and visited every home in my community and our satellite communities, and lo and behold, I was elected in February 2020. Of course I was asking myself, what have I gotten myself into – unbeknownst to me I had jumped into a lion's den of corruption, nepotism and politically driven favours that were rampant throughout an organization that just lost millions to theft. I know what you are thinking, because I thought the same thing!! On top of this, my trip to Jamaica was cancelled and I was navigating my way through a new position as a community leader, managing Human Resources full-time at my job and being a full-time mom. A hockey mom at that. Oh and did I mention there was a global pandemic? Easy peasy right? I mean what's hard about that? I can handle this.

As the world around us stood still and we all adapted to our new life of being home and finding our new normal to complete our tasks, it suddenly became clear that how we operate as women and our drive for success is so passionate and so overwhelmingly wonderful, that we nearly kill ourselves every day to be 'successful'. As I sat in my basement pondering why I am doing all of this, why am I working 35 hours a week, teaching my child from home, cooking dinner, taking care of my family and leading an entire population of underrepresented people? Why am I killing myself to help others? The only answer I could come up with was because I have to. Because I don't have a choice. Because something greater than me and you has brought me to where I am and why I am. If the pandemic has brought any good, it has allowed families to slow down and see the good in what they have at home.

Things were slowing down. I was getting used to helping my son navigate his schoolwork at home. I was trying to figure out a way to help him, as he had been newly diagnosed with dyslexia. He was going to be starting a new school this year to help him with his learning disability. We were excited to have a professional teach him new ways of learning. He was excited to go to a new learning centre where he wouldn't feel judged. COVID-19 took that learning centre from us. As a small business, they had to close due to COVID-19 and the lack of students and money. We had to start looking for new ways for my son to learn. What's a little more stress, right? I can handle this.

Then just as we seemingly started to get used to our new normal, our tiny province was torn to shreds by a sociopath who murdered 23 unsuspecting individuals. I remember clearly the events – as I frantically tried to contact my child's father, being just 30 minutes from the shooting I was terrified he may head towards them and find them asleep in their beds. My mind was racing, my heart was pounding, no one was answering. As the events unfolded, I was panicked and terrified – had he already found them? Were they okay? Exhausted and teary-eyed I fell asleep with my phone in my hand, praying they were unharmed. Unlike so many others, my family called me in the morning. I was lucky. Many people I know were affected by this tragedy. Many lives will never be the same. Nova Scotia, as a whole will never look at an RCMP vehicle without a shudder of remembrance. It was a horrific event that brought the entire world together in empathy, sympathy and compassion. Campaigns were made, money was donated, grieving families were supported physically, mentally and emotionally by the rest of the world. Little Nova Scotia will forever be remembered as the tiny east coast province that came together in a time of need and supported each other through the most difficult tragedy to ever occur on Canadian soil. I can handle this.

As the shock and horror began to dissipate and our Atlantic Bubble opened up to allow some freedom from the rigors of Public Health and Safety qualms, life seemingly started to quiet as we hoped to have a somewhat enjoyable summer. We prayed that our efforts to keep COVID-19 off our doorstep were enough to at least enjoy the nice weather. Fortunately, it proved to be a decent summer where the outdoors was enjoyed, small gatherings were permitted and our lives returned to a more normal state than we had become accustomed to over the past few months. Of course in 2020 style, that was to be short lived. Throughout the summer months some First Nation's communities had been participating in and working on Moderate Livelihood fishing plans to implement within their communities to access their inherent Treaty Rights.

On September 17, the anniversary of the Donald Marshall Junior Supreme Court ruling, Sipekne'katik First Nation launched their Moderate Livelihood Fishery and gave their fishers tags under this program. Non-Native commercial fishers were outraged and started a campaign to lobby government to force the Indigenous fishers to fish within seasons regulated by the Department of Fisheries and Oceans (DFO) Canada. Unfortunately things got heated and racism began to rear its ugly head. So, on top of a global pandemic and a mass shooting, we now have racist asshats burning down buildings and vehicles and assaulting people over a court affirmed inherent right, that they disagree with. I know it sounds ridiculous and you are probably wondering what this has to do with me? My spouse is an Indigenous man. An Indigenous commercial fisherman, who makes his living in a DFO regulated season. I run his company for him – so naturally I order traps, bait bags, fuel, you name it – that's my job. When the 2020 fishing season began, I went about business as usual and tried to order traps from a local business we use regularly. When I called, I knew something was happening, something was off. When the store clerk told me he "wasn't able to order or sell me traps because I am Indigenous", I almost fell off my chair. Let's be candid, I have been dealing with racism my entire life. I have always been the white girl or people would say "you're white, look at your skin, you're not native", but for the first time in my life I was discriminated against and denied a service because I was Indigenous. It hurt. I was angered and distraught. For the first time in my life I had experienced what my people go through on a daily basis. As you grow up within an Indigenous community you understand the barriers and hardships Indigenous people face. It isn't until you have actually experienced them, that you have the ability to comprehend the feeling. That is privilege. For those of you in the back who don't know what it is, privilege is not having to wonder if you will be serviced, not having to wonder if you will be followed, not having to wonder if you will be treated justly because of your race, ethnicity, or simply the colour of your skin. It's being entitled to all the good things without being an exception, it's being considered a human before 2011. Did y'all know Indigenous people couldn't file a human rights complaint before 2011, because we were still considered wards of the state? In 2011 – that is not a typo, 2011. Yet non-Indigenous folks get upset when they are called settlers or colonizers.  No we don't think you should pay for what your ancestors did to ours – but we do hope you can stop acting shitty and realize that everything you have in this province is because it was forced from our control. We also want you to realize that this land is ours, it has never been surrendered nor will it ever be. We also want you to know that you have no title to the land or its resources – we do. If we want to exercise our rights it is not a commercial problem, it is not an industry problem, it is not a DFO problem and it is not a government problem. It IS our right and you need to stop imposing your privilege and notion of entitlement upon it. Sure, it affects your livelihood, but you have been affecting ours for hundreds of years.

Throughout all of this turmoil I have had to watch my spouse walk into the fire to continue to provide for our family. It is gut-wrenching to think that he could be a target of racism in 2020. It has also been hard to swallow that our province has not come together to support their Indigenous brothers and sisters during their time of crisis. I hope this will change in the future and more allies will stand strong with our nation. I can handle this.

Needless to say, 2020 has been a rough year, it has shown us that we need to slow down, and we need to respect each other. It has shown us that our organizations and institutions need to do better to protect us and to be accountable for their actions.

I have never contemplated what 2020 has been like for me. I have never sat down and tried to verbalize or comprehend what has happened over the last 12 months. Maybe because I do not have time to do that, or maybe because I simply would rather not. What I do know is, I have learned a lot, I have endured a lot and I have succeeded tremendously. I have learned that no matter what aversion or obstacle stands in my way, I am strong, I am resilient, and I am unbreakable. I can handle this.

I have learned that the most important part of life is not your career or the money in your bank account, it is the people in your corner and the good you do with your voice. We can all hold a title that is important but what we choose to do with that title defines who we are as individuals, as leaders and as women. Sometimes doing the right thing feels like shit and that is why most people choose to sit on the fence rather than be accountable – 2020 has also taught me that silence can be perceived as status quo but being present when it matters most is louder than any spoken word. I can handle this.

Somehow, throughout this godforsaken journey I have found some purpose. I have taken the hard topics head-on and shattered the glass ceiling that was holding me down. I have become a successful Indigenous leader within my community and I am proud to be accountable and transparent to my constituents. I left my full-time job because I was not satisfied emotionally and realized that it is okay to make moves to better my own wellness. It is okay to feel crappy about holding people accountable. Most importantly, I have come to understand that it is okay to take a step back and see the bigger picture. It is okay to need more information. It is okay to throw out the trash to move forward as a community, as a leader and as an individual. I can handle this.

## About Carley Gloade

Carley was born and raised in the Millbrook First Nation, she has a strong passion for driving her community forward and being a strong advocate for indigenous people as a whole but specifically for the members of her home community.

Aside from her position on the Millbrook Chief and Council, Carley is the Vice Chair of the Nova Scotia Career Development Association Board of Directors. Carley attended Saint Mary's University to obtain a bachelor's degree with a Major in Sociology and a Minor in Religious Studies. She continued her education via NSCC and enrolled in Interdisciplinary Studies with a focus in Non-Profit Management and later at Dalhousie University in Career Development Services Level I and II. Carley worked for the Millbrook First Nation for 10 years as the Native Employment Officer, the Native Employment Office Coordinator and the Receptionist.

Carley is an avid athlete and participates in sports regularly. She has been playing competitive volleyball for 23 years, has won two NSSAF Tier 1 Championships, multiple Club Championships and is a part of the reigning 7-year champions of the Nova Scotia Mi'kmaq Summer Games Women's Volleyball team. Carley was also avid in Track & Field and won three Provincial titles in the 80 m hurdles and set a regional record for the fastest 80 m hurdles sprint on a dirt track in 1998. Carley is currently the volleyball coach for the Nova Scotia Mi'kmaq

Summer Games Millbrook Female volleyball teams, North American Indigenous Games U19 Female Volleyball Team and the former, U15 Truro Cougars Assistant Coach, who were the 2019 Provincial champions in their division.

# COLLEEN O'DEA

RESILIENT • INSPIRING • CREATIVE • GENUINE • FUNNY

I knew this year would challenge me. I'd reflected on it and reached the consensus that it was up to me to make it better. Up to me, to get out of my head and push through.

The thing is... this wasn't the first time I'd faced a challenge... and it likely wouldn't be the last.

My challenge... my nest had emptied.

As a mom who put her children first through her divorce... even when I'd returned to school in my forties and started a new career... their needs came before everything else. It was my utmost joy to be their mom and I created a career where I could be at every tournament, game, and field trip... where I could drop anything at a moment's notice to be there for them. It was my privilege to raise them... and I was proud of all I'd done.

A few months before we rang in the new year, my two youngest flew from the nest to begin the next chapter of their lives, I'd sold our family home to move into an apartment and start the next chapter of mine... and just after the holidays, my oldest moved to Spain to start a new chapter as well.

We were all moving forward and as I reflected with a heavy heart... I knew I needed to make big changes to go from being the mom who was there 100% of the time... to a mom who needed to reinvent and put herself first for the first time in decades!

I decided, that I would face 2020 and be DARING. That I would attempt Twenty New Adventures in 2020... that I would start online dating and really and truly, push myself out of my comfort zone to discover who I was... now that "mom" was no longer my number one role.

2020 began with a trip to Florida with friends... where I worked poolside, enjoyed some shopping and dining... and tested the waters to see what "snow bird" could look like. I came home relaxed and refreshed with a sense of what my entrepreneurial life could look like... where I had this job that once allowed me to be there for my kids as much as possible... and would now allow me to live a life a bit more selfishly.

Within a week of arriving home, I was ill. A chest cold that wouldn't let up... I lowered my head and spent the time relaxing at home... in my beautiful apartment... taking much needed rest breaks and even spending full days in bed. By the end of February, I was feeling much better and as I was set to celebrate my youngest turning 20... we'd opted to have a family party at home, rather than hitting up a pub, as I was just getting my energy back and my daughter insisted I needed more rest.

Little did I know... that would be the last time I'd see my family for months.

When the pandemic and lockdown began, I was all in. As much as I missed my children, I knew my health came first... I settled into cozy clothes, puzzles and Zoom calls, online groceries, and wine deliveries. I worried about my children... most especially, about my oldest in Spain. But all three assured me they were fine... they needed to not see me... they needed me to put myself first and avoid getting sick (though on reflection, I question whether I'd already had Covid in February!)

While I was trying my best to keep my spirits up, despite not being able to be with friends and family, Nova Scotia was hit with a mass shooting that was simply too much to bear.

Days turned into weeks of watching daily news updates... following along on social media in complete disbelief. As a province, we were shaken beyond imagination.

2020 was about as brutal as one could imagine... folks weren't able to be with loved ones sick in hospital, funerals weren't able to be held, a friend wasn't able to fly to India to adopt the child they'd waited so long for, businesses were going under in ridiculous numbers...

I was feeling it all.

That beautiful apartment I was so proud of became my "pretty bunker." Loneliness was overwhelming and I was feeling this empty nest, far more empty than I'd anticipated when the year began.

There were a few highlights.

My children visited from the doorway... brought treats, groceries, flowers, and love... though not being able to hug them was an ache I'd never known existed.

I got a cat... much to the surprise of everyone as I'd only had dogs in the past, I welcomed a cat into my home and have been unexpectedly thrilled!

I spent time with friends and family... online. Enjoying a few drinks with friends on the weekends, Sunday family time, teas and chats in the afternoon with colleagues.

I "pivoted" my business successfully... a business that began falling apart and had me flying through my savings... is now on its feet. I took every free online course imaginable and was ever so thankful to those who offered them up! I focused on what I could control. Attended conferences and meetings. And in time, watched things turn around.

By summer, I began spending time with friends outside,

in our small bubble, as numbers in Nova Scotia remained low and I felt more confident going out.

I hugged my children.

2020...the year I was to be DARING, the year of ADVENTURES and discovering who I was... did not, in any way, meet my expectations.

But it's temporary. Others have it far worse than I did. Perspective is a wonderful thing.

2020 has made me realize what's most important in my life. It's made me reevaluate my expectations. It's made me incredibly grateful for the things I have.

I spent much of this year having to whack myself in the head... to remind myself that it could have been worse. That I'm surrounded by love. That my parents are doing well. That I have this fabulous apartment. That I had savings to pull me through. That I didn't lose my career. That I have three children who absolutely adore me.

Nightly, I say my prayers and I think of the people who lost so much in 2020 and send them all of the positive thoughts that I can.

I cannot tell you the number of times when I'd felt over-whelmed with not being able to see my children, that I was reminded of my friends who'd waited for years to adopt a child, finally had everything in order, had his room decorated and ready to welcome him home... and at the last moment, were shut down by Covid.

However, just as the year is coming to a close... and as I write this piece... these beautiful people got on a flight, and finally wrapped their arms around their precious little boy.

There are better days ahead... days where we'll head out on big adventures and be more daring... but for now, humanity requires that we scale things back for the sake of each and every one of us. So that one day, we'll live with the same sense of freedom that we took for granted.

Where we'll be forever grateful... for everything we have.

———

## About Colleen O'Dea

Colleen O'Dea is a social influencer and the storyteller behind her lifestyle blog, Curtains are Open. Colleen writes from the heart, always showing her vulnerable side, quite often with a touch of humour. Colleen is a Graphic Designer and sells many of her designs through her Etsy shop, Drawbridge Creative. She is the proud mom of three adult children, is single and empty nesting in her 50s, and most recently... she got a cat.

www.curtainsareopen.com
IG at @queenofcurtains

# DIANE MUISE

HAPPY • FUNNY • STRONG • INDEPENDENT • LOVING • FAITHFUL • KIND

Always keep going...

Life isn't fair. There are no guarantees in life. Life is short. While all of these things are true the most important thing is to remember that your life is what you make it.

2020 started out as an amazing year for me. I got engaged on a cruise ship somewhere on the ocean between Cozumel and Belize. I was going to marry the love of my life. I had been married before 30 years ago and had three boys who I ended up raising as a single parent. It wasn't easy but it was worth it. The saying, "What doesn't kill you makes you stronger," meant I should have been superwoman. Or that God only gives you what you can handle, he obviously had more faith in my abilities than I did. But, I kept going.

March started like any other March but then it derailed. Covid-19 had hit Nova Scotia and we as a province were shocked, scared, angry and unhinged. I went to stay with my Mum. I didn't know much about what was going on but I knew I didn't want my 82 year old mother living alone. I was grateful we had a house to live in, thankful I could work from home and blessed that we were healthy. I felt fortunate.

Then our beloved Nova Scotia exploded. Nothing we could have expected or imagined happened; a monster was loose. For two days he killed and destroyed lives. So sickening, so sad, so heart-wrenching. I noticed a post a friend had made so I messaged her. She said call me. It was then that I knew, before I called her, I already knew. I had lost one of my best friends. How could that have happened? I had just talked to her. I had just messaged her. The tears ran down my face as the understanding that I would never see her again began to sink in. She was ripped from our lives! I was angry. I was hurt. I was sad.

Gina was so full of life. We laughed so much. We had so much fun! We might have even gotten into trouble now and then. She was stubborn, strong, and fiercely independent. Maybe there was a reason she didn't put off doing all the things she wanted to do. Maybe, somehow, she knew she didn't have that many tomorrows. We all should live like we have limited tomorrows. Health and happiness, family and friends, adventures and memories, these are what matter most.

I spent many hours, reliving in my mind all of our adventures, and there were so many. I would smile as the tears escaped and slid down my cheeks. The hours turned to days and the days turned to weeks. I had to begin to focus on other things. I had to keep going.

Then my heart was ripped apart again before it had time to heal. I lost my favorite girl, my Abby. She had been at my side for almost 11 years. She was always happy, wagging her tail, and running to see me and getting a lick in some-where. She was my most faithful friend. It was my turn to look after her and I could not let her suffer. I had to let her go. My world was crashing; my girl was gone. I still look for her, think about her often and miss her always. But, I had to keep going.

A missing child, many military personnel who had died on duty, children becoming orphans, parents becoming childless and people dying in hospitals all alone. So much tragedy, so much hurt. When would it stop? We need to remember.

We need to remember the little things that are important to us, the memories we have created and have the desire to make the most of the life that we have been given. That doesn't mean you won't get hurt, that you won't be angry, sad or scared, that tragedy still won't find you. But you keep going. You may have days that you are mad at the world, but don't let those days turn into weeks. You might have days that you are so depressed that you can't stop crying or get out of bed. But, the next day, put a smile on your face, get out of bed and face the world. Ask for help; everyone needs help sometime. Always keep going.

Be kind to each other, have faith in what you believe, hope for a better tomorrow but live for today, and love with all your heart. Empty that bucket list today, don't wait for all the tomorrows that may never come. Always keep going...

## About Diane Muise

Diane Muise grew up on a farm and was no stranger to hard work. Following in her grandmother's footsteps, she became a teacher and has taught math to junior and senior high students for 24 years. During this time she raised 3 boys and now has 5 grand-babies, all under 5 years old. She loves rug hooking and making crafts of many types. She will retire in June 2021, and is looking forward to the next chapter in her life including marrying Brian, the love of her life, in August 2021. Just keep going...

# EMILY KIERSTEAD

A COMPOSER OF MUSIC • CREATIVE • VIVACIOUS
COMPASSIONATE • GREGARIOUS

"I will be there when you need me
though we're very far apart
I will be right there beside you
You will find me in your heart."
– DONNA RHODENIZER

My grand-daughter and her choir sang this beautiful song in a concert in March. It now echoes in my mind, as three weeks after this performance, her mother was brutally murdered in Portapique. The acts of a mentally disturbed man who was paranoid about Covid-19 sent ripples of grief through the families of twenty-two people, and caused the province of Nova Scotia to spiral into an abyss of disbelief and horror.

I am grateful to be asked to write about my daughter, Lisa McCully.

These will be some of my cherished memories of my

middle child. A tall, beautiful, and vivacious young woman, Lisa found that each day offered an adventure. Even as a child she was spilling over with accounts of her "wonderful" day at school. Whether it be through travelling, or in teaching elementary children, or mothering her own two young offspring, she lived life to 200%.

Lisa grew up in Quispamsis, N.B., excelling in swimming, piano, and school leadership. In her High School of 2,000 students, she was a capable President of the Student Council. Her summer vacations took her to work in Cavendish, PEI, or south to the Dominican Republic to live with a family in the mountains. There she enhanced her Spanish, shared her room with three children and four pigs who wandered in and out through the night. With Rufino, her host, she travelled up the mountain, picking up union members until the back of the ½-ton truck was full. From Rufino, who was the head of the coffee-growers union in that area, she learned much about distributive justice.

Upon attending Mount Allison University, Lisa became an avid rugby player, and often watched football games with her sister and brother who hitchhiked to Mount A. from their respective universities for a game. Her language studies took her to Strasbourg, France, where she would be totally immersed in the French language.

That was when I was invited to join her to backpack around Europe before she returned to Canada. One night on the Euro-Rail, we shared a "couchette" with three men. Lisa whispered from her bunk above me "Don't anger them, Mom, they are drug dealers from Columbia." No, mother did not sleep that night.

Backpacking around Europe! Lisa had brought her guitar with her, so we could busk on a street-corner of Baden-Baden, or sing up on a hill in Austria, so nearby strollers could enjoy songs in English and Spanish. We made enough money to buy ourselves a cup of coffee and a huge piece of Black Forest

Cake. Lisa had organized the trip (without email at that time) so that we knew what our lodgings would be each night, and when to catch the train for the next city, or country.

Back in Canada. The West Coast beckoned to both Lisa and her younger sister Jenny. They had a hilarious drive in a little VW across Canada to teaching positions in Vancouver. My letter from her reads "I have never laughed so much, I have never cried so much. This has been a marvellous trip."

Of course the girls made great friends. Of course, they poured their creativity into their teaching jobs. Both were lured to the concept of outdoor education and learning through activity. On the way home to N.S. where I had settled, Lisa stopped off in Toronto to teach for two years. (Her school Principal has contacted me, and we have become great email friends.) Playing Poker one night for the first time, she won the game and also the eye of Stuart, who happened to be from Parrsboro. Eventually they journeyed back to the "Far East," were married and settled in Parrsboro. A few years later, Lisa found herself to be a single mother of two active children. They will remember baking bread with their Mom, hunting for edible mushrooms, building a labyrinth on the side lawn of their large property, and other things too numerous to mention.

Lisa's students, whom she has taught from Advocate to Masstown to Debert, will have the conviction that here was an exceptional teacher, who loved each individual and worked diligently to equip them to live in this troubled world.

As Covid-19 descended on the world, Lisa used her expertise on the computer to assist other teachers in getting their lessons onto Zoom. She had offered to help any who needed advice, and shared her skills and her wisdom.

APRIL 2020

There are several children and many grown ups who are

grieving the senseless loss of a parent or family member. "Nova Scotia Strong" has become a logo to remind the residents of this province that arms and hearts are open in support of our twenty-two families who have been touched by tragedy.

My thoughts are with the R.C.M.P. who arrived on the horrific scene near midnight, knowing there was a shooter on the loose. Homes had been set on fire, and people had died. Our grandchildren and two other children were protected by four R.C.M.P. officers who stood guard at each corner of Lisa's large home. Untold courage needs applauding.

Much is said about mental health in this time of Covid-19. We need, each of us, to care for our neighbours and ourselves, to be political about gun control, and to act when we suspect dangerous behaviour. The quality of parenting and teaching cannot be undervalued. These are the men and women who form our future. These are the adults who make the difference between a stable, empathetic future generation, or a chaotic, mentally disturbed or narcissistic age in which innocent children will be harmed.

Support during a time of grief is vital. Don and I and my youngest daughter Jenny have been inundated with cards, letters of condolence, and quilts from groups across Canada. I have a dear friend who emails me every Saturday, and my brother calls that evening, to help me get through another reminder of the horrific events of that Saturday in April. Now Jenny is left to grieve both her brother and sister. A noted trainer of Yoga teachers, Jenny has been an impressive voice for our family both with the many media interviews, and with her very spiritual expression of living in this world.

How does one go on, to live as an almost eighty year old who would gladly give her life that Lisa might continue her vibrant journey on earth? Mine is a compounded grief, with my son Jonathan's death from cancer three years ago. Counselling has offered ways in which to navigate the grief journey. Victim Services of Nova Scotia has been very helpful. Friends have held me, though often virtually, strangers have reached out in empathy from as far as the West Coast, the U.S. and Europe. There was a letter of condolence from a lovely woman in Sweden who read about the massacre and wanted to express her love to the families.

I will survive because of precious grandchildren. I will live for them, and for the gratitude of having given birth to such incredibly elegant and talented human beings. Lisa is with me, has moved from being a physical presence to a firm soul who is embedded in my heart and mind. I hear her laughter, her words, "Let your faith be bigger than your fear," and her singing, daily. I treasure the text video that she sent me on April 16th. Lisa, dressed in black, was dancing with abandonment across her large living room, swirling to the music, and swishing her beautiful blond hair to the rhythm.

Yesterday I was restringing my violin, using a flash-light to see the intricate winding of strings around the pegs at the end of the neck. As I paused for a moment, the flashlight eerily focused on a beautiful picture of a smiling Lisa across the room. I could hear her in my mind, saying: "Keep on, Mum. Let your faith be stronger than your fear." Yes, my darling Lisa, thank you for all you have given to me and to the world.

Lisa's Facebook entry a few days before her death read:

"The Human Spirit

is

Stronger

than

Anything that

can happen to it."

## About Emily Kierstead

Emily Kierstead is a retired United Church Minister and Teacher living in Truro, N.S. She lived much of her life in southern New Brunswick, where she served in churches in Fredericton, Saint John and Rothesay. When her children were young, she taught Elementary School Music so that her weekends would be free. On moving to N.S. she met and married Rev. Don Murray, and ministered in Middle Musquodoboit throughout the 90's.

# IFEOMA ESONWUNE

RESILIENT • CREATIVE • DYNAMIC • VISIONARY
ENTHUSIASTIC • RESULT ORIENTED

## MY STORY OF PAIN, RESILIENCE, & RECOVERY

As I watched the clock tick down to midnight on Tuesday, December 31st, 2019 I counted every second of the last minute of the previous year and ushered in the new year 2020 with joy and enthusiasm. Once the celebrations had died down, I refocused my gaze on how to make 2020 the best year ever, personally and professionally, and girl, I was fired up.

2020 started as a typical year. I had set big SMART goals hoping to smash each one of them. I was enthusiastic, confident, energetic, and willing to give it my best to change the trajectory of my life and grow my business to the next level. I had curated a perfect diary for 2020. I reassured myself that this would be an ideal year, but little did I know that calamity was lurking at the corners. That "perfect" wasn't a choice word for 2020.

To state the obvious, it's been a rough year for everyone. But has also been a year of love, resilience and recovery for my Province of Nova Scotia and me. The random yet overwhelming series of unfortunate occurrences that characterize 2020 has helped me realize how far I have evolved as a person. How blessed I am to be Canadian and how beautiful it is to live in Nova Scotia.

Losing my dad in the middle of a global pandemic on Easter Sunday (04/12/2020) shattered my heart into a million pieces. I had barely begun to pick up the broken pieces of my heart when a week later (04/19/2020), Nova Scotia witnessed the worst mass shooting in Canadian history. My beautiful, peaceful, and vibrant Nova Scotia went dark with sorrow. No one could make sense of such a tragedy. No one could discern how one senseless wicked man could inflict so much pain on a loving and peaceful people.

The whole world was in a shutdown due to a global pandemic. My father died thousands of kilometres away from me, and I had no chance to bid him a final farewell. 22 innocent people lost their lives in the most senseless act of violence ever recorded in Canadian history. It was the most depressing moment of my life. I laid in my bed for most of each day and would cry myself to sleep every night. I felt helpless, looking for answers, but none were forthcoming. Heartbreak was painful enough without having to watch your children try so hard to understand why the person they look up to couldn't hold it together anymore. I was a nervous wreck and didn't think I would survive the trauma. I shut down, and daylight seemed like darkness.

Personally, the few months following my dad's death were hard. I struggled on, trying to keep my head above water. I took medications to help me fall and stay asleep. I was fatigued, and life made no sense anymore. It took some time, but I began to put the broken pieces of my heart together again. I began to mend and heal. And every time, it was the resilience, love, and the strength of friends and other Nova Scotians that kept me going.

It would take months before I began to feel alive again. It took a lot of love from my family and friends to bring me back to who I used to be. My husband and kids are my treasures for eternity. I was made better by the outpouring of love from friends. I was relieved to know that there was help out there whenever I needed it. Nova Scotia is the true meaning of love and strength. We bonded and healed as people together. I realized I was not alone in my pain. We are "#NovaScotiaStrong."

Eventually, I started to heal, but not me alone. Nova Scotia began to heal as well. Recovery is challenging and can be scary, but Nova Scotians made it seem effortless. Shortly after the senseless shooting, the #NovaScotiaStrong started, and extraordinary human beings, my fellow Nova Scotians, did not allow a tragedy to define us. So many people rose above and beyond to bring help to families affected and bring calm to our souls, sharing with the world the beauty, strength and love that make us Nova Scotians.

Reflecting on these experiences now is proof of one fact... that I am stronger than I think, and we are more powerful together. Six months ago, I had my worst breakdown. Six months later, I am grateful for who I am and who we are as a Province. I had witnessed us at our lowest point, but the pain and agony didn't define us. Our love and resilience outweighed the pain. Staying down wasn't an option for me anymore. So, I did everything I could to drag myself out of the hole of depression. Meditation helped me get my thoughts together. Before long, I felt strong enough to continue on the journey amidst all odds.

I still think about my dad every day, but I don't let the thoughts weigh me down anymore. I make sure to focus on the positive sides of our relationship, the beautiful moments we had together and the love we shared to bring up my mood. Sometimes it is difficult, but I force myself to focus on the brighter side of everything.

Despite 2020 being an unprecedented year, I've continued my work, impacting and empowering women and girls in my community, across Canada, and beyond. I have learned to talk about my mental health openly and comfortably. I've continued to share inspiring stories of amazing women worldwide through my Rise and Lead Women's Magazine. My story is positive, I survived, and I'm still recovering.

I have become more resilient, wiser, and open to challenges because I know that my struggles don't define me; my resilience does. My 2020 experiences contribute to who I am today and who I will continue to be in the future.

## About Ifeoma Esonwune

Ifeoma Esonwune is a Communication strategist, Entrepreneur, Speaker, Leadership coach, Event Planner, Community influencer, Storyteller, award winner and food enthusiast.

She is the Founder, Network for the Empowerment of Women. Founder & President, Little Learners Social Association. Publisher, Rise and Lead Women's Magazine. Owner, Matella Event Concepts and Co-Owner Atlantic Grubs Halifax.

Ifeoma collaborates with businesses to develop successful communication strategies and follow industry trends in assessing impacts of communication plans. She helps businesses generate new techniques to make business communication more effective.

Ifeoma is also devoted to empowering and helping women and girls discover their potentials and turn their passions into profitable business ventures. She loves to inspire and engage the children and youths in her community and around the world.

Ifeoma is the Creator, Inspire by Tales, a storytelling club that engages and inspires elementary school kids. She is also the creator, Rise and Lead Girls' Forum. Ifeoma loves to empower and amplify the voices of ordinary women and girls and provides a platform for them to discover themselves and utilize their innate talents to improve their lives.

Ifeoma's academic background is in Communication, Management and Leadership, and also in Strategic Planning, Hospitality, Sports and Leisure Management.

Ifeoma has won several awards and recognitions including the Most Inspiring Immigrant in the Maritime Award, Global News Morning Community Star Award etc. She has received recognitions and mentions in the Nova Scotian House of Assembly for her community works.

Ifeoma is passionate about diversity, inclusion and the growth and equality of women in business and leadership.

# JOSIE RYAN

RESOURCEFUL • HUMBLE • DRIVEN • COMPASSIONATE • FAIR

## WHEN I GO QUIET

Taking a minute to reflect on 2020 brings great emotions, many which are generally tucked away inside me. I have been a Registered Nurse for over 35 years and held leadership roles for most of my career. 2020 has drawn on all my experiences and coping strategies. I began my career in Long Term Care 30 years ago and never looked back. I love doing what I do, it is a part of who I am both personally and emotionally. Getting to know people, building relationships by truly caring and respecting them is so important to me. As a leader, ensuring residents are the core of every decision and seeking to understand the people who care and support them has been a priority. All of this has made the tragedy of the coronavirus so overwhelming and had such a deep impact on me.

51

The emotions of the past 9 months have been intense, going from fear, to adrenaline rushes, to a feeling of sheer paralysis. I drew on the love and passion I have for long term care and on the goal to create an environment for seniors where they are valued for their life long contributions and where the wisdom of their past and experiences are celebrated. A home where they can continue to live and contribute within a community.

We celebrate the birth of baby and it is such a joyous occasion but there is no greater honour than to be given the privilege to hold the hand of a person as they leave this world. To be able to bring comfort and to let someone know they made a difference and are loved as they end this part of their journey. That is truly amazing.

In the summer of 2019, I sat at my cottage looking out over the beauty of the river and I remember saying to myself "hold on to this image, you are going to need it"! I didn't know why at the time nor could I have imagined just how many times I would rely on that vision. Remember there is still peace and beauty in the world.

When COVID-19 was discovered in the facility the entire Northwood community reacted. Everyone had worked so hard to prevent the virus from entering the facility that there was a sense of shock and sadness yet so many showed up determined and ready for battle.

For me the most difficult part was the judgement by so many who were looking from the outside. We were struggling to cope with an illness that was new with many unknowns and, every day, as we learned more, we responded. When laboratory results came in each morning they brought such emotion as faces and relationships flooded of people I knew. Having to share the information invoked those same emotions in the entire team knowing the fear and uncertainty that a positive test brought to residents, their families and staff.

Watching or listening to news casts and reporters became overwhelming, there was never an escape. While people wanted all the details we were living it. It was difficult to hear information that was not accurate but it was even tougher to help staff stay positive when every day they selflessly came to care for residents. People who were afraid for their own health and their families showing up and doing what they do best, giving their all. Everyone wore their mask yet their eyes were a window into their fatigue, their determination and their desire in doing what they do best... caring for others.

It was important for me to be there, to be visible, to support and be a part of the team. I couldn't be anywhere else. My husband was my life line and he took care of me. I would come home late in the evening, take off my work clothes in the laundry room, place them in the washer, then take a shower before connecting with anyone. Dinner was always ready so we could spend a few minutes together and then I would start to work again usually until early morning hours and the phone would start ringing by 7 a.m. again. This continued for weeks for so many of us.

There are no words to express the gratitude for the support we received from across Nova Scotia. The calls, cards and emails I received from so many people I have known throughout my career. They will never know what their words of encouragement or empathy meant and how many days it was those few words that gave me strength to move on to another day. I remember standing outside as cars drove by and people cheered and shouted support for staff and Northwood, it was so overpowering and made my heart race and it was difficult to breathe. I saw hope and pride on the faces of staff that I had not seen for weeks.

When I go quiet is when the experience floods back. I can recall the events so vividly... the emotions, sadness, fear, anger for the hurt and loss and yet thankfulness, compassion, pride and gratitude for the strength and compassion shown by so many. There has not been a day or night that it does not creep into my thoughts, when I go quiet.

Although this wave, or more like tsunami, has washed over us, the fear and anxiety remains as the virus is still here, there is still no vaccine, and still limited treatment for those so vulnerable. We continue to prepare with what we learned, prepare for responding to the unknown, prepare for wave 2, for wave 3. Can I continue, or can we do it again? Am I physically, mentally and emotionally strong enough to help lead through this again? I ask myself those questions every day and every day I show up because people count on me, because there is a reason I became a nurse, because I have the desire to lead and because I still have the passion to care. Because at Northwood we have the power of love!

## About Josie Ryan

As the executive director of long-term care and a member of the Corporate Leadership Team for the Northwood Group of Companies, Josie leads a multidisciplinary clinical team providing compassionate, high quality continuing care services for 730 long-term care residents across three urban and rural sites. Josie is the former Director of Organizational Health for Northwood, where she was responsible for occupational health, infection control, workplace safety, attendance management, and promotion of a healthy workplace. Previously with Northwood, Josie has worked to ensure the safety of residents and staff as Infection Control Coordinator/Manager and Occupational Health Nurse. Prior to her leadership at Northwood, Josie was the Associate Director of Care at Shannex and an Acting Head Nurse in Outpatient/Emergency at Moose Factory General Hospital. Josie holds a Masters Certification in Health Care Leadership from Cornell University, Certification in Occupational Health Nursing from MacEwen University, past Certification in Infection Control from CBIC, a Certificate in Business Management from Dalhousie University and a Diploma in Nursing from Saint Rita School of Nursing.

# KAREN DEAN

FIERCE LEADER • RESILIENT SURVIVOR • PASSIONATE MOM
POSITIVE THINKER • GRATEFUL GIVER

2020 was going to be *my year*.

Yep. That's what I said back in 2019. Not only did I say it out loud (to absolutely everyone who would listen), but I posted it all over social media too... you know... to keep my self account-able... and, if it is on social media, it has to be true, right?!

This was my year to travel, to meet new people, to take my business to the next level. Hell, I was going to skip a few levels and maybe, just maybe, hit 7-figures in revenue. I had some seriously huge goals. I hired the most amazing coach – a fierce business woman who I have admired for years, who has built a 7-figure business herself while living in rural Nova Scotia. I could finally afford to hire her! I finally felt like I deserved to be part of one of her prestigious programs. I was finally sitting in the same room with her and so many other absolutely incredible female entrepreneurs. It was everything I had dreamed of! (Note – if you want to reach huge goals, you always need to hang out with people who are more successful than you and soak up all of the knowledge you can from them!)

This was the year I wasn't going to be "_____'s mom"... pick a name... I have 3 kids. I gave up being "_____'s wife" years ago (two divorces ... but that's another book!) Now I was ME! I was Karen. I could even look past the fact that every derogatory meme on the planet used the name Karen for the female character (I considered changing my name. I have always hated my name but I am kinda used to it now. And that seemed a little harsh. But, while we are on the subject... ladies, can we do more building each other up instead of trying to knock each other down with derogatory memes?)

Back to my story... I went on one incredible trip at the end of January. I had never been "down south" before and I had the opportunity to go to a business retreat at a beautiful resort in Mexico with my business coach and a cohort of other powerhouse women in business. I summoned every bit of courage I had and boarded a plane for Cancun BY MYSELF and then took an hour-long taxi ride to the resort, again BY MYSELF. My kids were making plans for what they were going to do with the life insurance payout when I died alone in Mexico... but I digress. What an experience it was to be in the company of so many like-minded women, and in such a gorgeous place! You could feel the powerful energy in the room. The discussions were so inspiring and lifelong friendships were made. For the first time in my life, I had taken time for myself and my own goals, not goals that were attached to a man or to one or all of my kids. I actually relaxed and didn't worry about what might be happening at home, trusting that the plan I had in place was working and that everyone at home was being well looked after. That was a huge deal for me... I am bit of a worrier and tend to be kind of a control freak when it comes to my home and my children.

I came home with so many brilliant ideas for my business and immediately started the process of implementation. This is what I was meant to do. I had never felt so alive. I was a guest on podcasts. I spoke at events. I was asked to host a live show online. People asked mutual connections to introduce them to me because they follow me on social media and I inspired them so much that they couldn't wait to meet me in person. ME??!! Say WHAT??!! Karen Dean, the country girl, single mom, who lives in the boonies??!! They want to meet me??!!

Dreams do come true. I have firmly believed for years that all of the shit that I have been through, and thrived through, happened for a reason. I came to the conclusion that it all happened so that I could inspire others when they felt like their best life was out of their reach. Because, NEWSFLASH, the only thing standing between you and your best life is YOU! And I had been standing in my own way for far too many years.

Then, in the blink of an eye, Covid-19 started to rain on my parade. Like, monsoon rains. The world shut down. Literally. Entire countries came to a standstill. Planes were grounded. Schools were closed. Churches were closed. Borders were closed. Everything as we knew it shut down. Then I shut down. I went into a cocoon of solitude and fear. Never had I felt so unsafe in my life... and, trust me, I have felt pretty damn unsafe on many occasions. But this was different. I didn't know how to protect myself and my children from something I couldn't see. The media was basically telling us that we were all going to die from this dreaded new virus, it was just a matter of when. The fear instilled in all of us was real. And, all of the sudden, my kids and I were all stuck in a house together. And no one could go anywhere! I mean, I love my kids beyond words, but every mama needs a break sometimes!

And masks! We are all supposed to wear masks? I have never worn a mask in my life, except those awful 1980s plastic Halloween masks! But, you couldn't even buy masks. Every store everywhere was out of stock! And hand sanitizer and toilet paper were nowhere to be found. I will never understand the toilet paper hoarding but... suddenly things we never thought about before were the first thing we thought about every day!

And lonely... can we just talk about how lonely it is to be the only adult in a house? I mean, I am used to being a single parent. It has been 9 years now. But the loneliness hit hard when I knew there was no chance in hell of me meeting a potential partner since I couldn't leave my property! And even my friends weren't allowed to come visit. Loneliness is not a feeling that I am very familiar with and I didn't like it.

After a few weeks things started to get easier. This "new normal" wasn't so bad. I began to appreciate being forced to stay home and enjoy my beautiful piece of paradise. I could get back to my focus of growing my business and making my dreams come true. That is what 2020 was supposed to be about. There was still time to make it all happen!

Then, THEN, on April 18 and 19, a crazed killer drove through our beautiful, peaceful province and took the lives of 22 innocent people, plus an unborn baby. His last victim was a dear friend of mine.

I got the call at around 7:30 pm from another friend. I could barely understand her through her sobbing, "Gina, he got Gina!"

*Nooooo!! No!! Not Gina! I was going to text her this morning and tell her to come to my house because I had a bad feeling. But I didn't text her!!!! Why didn't I text her? She has survived cancer. Twice! This is not how she's gone! She was a single mom who would do anything for anyone! NOOOOO!!! She can't be gone!*

I couldn't believe what I was hearing. Gina was such an amazing person, a bright light in an often dark world. She was always smiling. She was always leaping, not just stepping, outside of her comfort zone. She was bold, fierce and kind. She was the type of person who you felt enter a room before you saw her. She had such an incredible presence and energy. She couldn't have left the world in this way!

All I could manage to do was sit on my couch and cry for a few days. I was obsessed with reading news stories as the media tried to piece together this horrible tragedy. And things just kept getting worse as we learned that there were 22 innocent lives taken and then we hear that one of the beautiful souls taken was pregnant and hadn't even had a chance to announce the news to her family yet. Life just wasn't fair. Suddenly all the media was talking about was "the worst mass shooting in Canadian history" and it happened here – in our quiet little province, in places where I go on a regular basis, in tiny villages where everyone knows everyone. This kind of thing doesn't happen in Nova Scotia. We leave our doors unlocked. We invite strangers into our homes and offer them a hot meal. We are known worldwide as being some of the nicest people on the planet. Mass shootings just don't happen here!

Then, one morning I could hear Gina's voice telling me to get up and do something, with a few added swear words, because that's Gina. The world needed me to do something. I have had a home-based online clothing company, Countryfied Clothing, since 2010 so the answer came to me quickly – a fundraiser, a clothing fundraiser, and I would donate 100% of the profit to the families and communities affected. Within hours I had it set up. I contacted the printing company that I use and we developed a Nova Scotia Strong design that I hoped would sell well. I bought a domain name. I designed the website and had it up and running in less than 4 hours. Then, I set what I thought was a reasonable goal of a $10,000 donation.

That wasn't enough for Gina. As it turned out, I had the opportunity to go on national television twice to tell the world how amazing Gina was. I took advantage of those opportunities to talk about my fundraiser – even though I wasn't really supposed to, but they can't really stop you once you start talking on live television – Gina isn't the only bold one! Immediately following those television appearances, orders started pouring in. We made $10,000 in one weekend!

Following that I set a new goal. In true Gina spirit, I thought big – $100,000!! My business had never made that much profit in a year ever before, but, why not?! That goal kept me working 16-18 hour days for over two months. Due to the Covid-19 restrictions, I wasn't able to have a large group of people to help process orders so it was essentially me and my kids and one amazing friend who did the majority of the work. I was grateful for some other friends who came for a day here and there to help out as well. I couldn't have done it without all of them. I poured my heart out on Facebook live videos every week to give updates on the fundraiser. I used every free marketing tool I could think of. And it worked – almost!  Little did I know that life as I knew it was about to shatter once again.

On June 27, my only son went to the doctor by himself for the first time ever – thanks to the Covid-19 restrictions I wasn't allowed to go with him. He had a weird cough for a while and had been getting short of breath at work.  It took me way too long to convince him that he needed to go to the doctor… teenagers often think that they are invincible.  He was at the emergency room all day. My daughter works at the hospital so she was able to pop in every now and then to check in with him. However, she was not in the room when the doctor came in to tell my 19-year old son, my baby boy, that he had a very large tumour in his chest that was most likely cancer!

Too many hours had passed of me worrying about what was going on at the hospital when my daughter finally called me from my son's bedside to tell me that he had a very large mass in his chest that the doctors believed to be a type of lymphoma. *What?! No! Not my boy! Can you repeat that? I don't think I heard you correctly! Lymphoma! That is cancer! My son can NOT have cancer! And my 22-year old daughter should not be the person who has to tell me that he might! I should be there with them!! 2020 – what the fuck??!!*

Three short days later we were at another hospital and he was having a chest biopsy. They stuck a needle in my son's chest… my poor boy. So many things could go wrong. And what made that experience even worse was that, thanks to the Covid-19 restrictions, I couldn't even be in the hospital with him! I consider myself a pretty strong mama who can handle anything but, that day, I cried. I cried in front of nurses when they asked me to leave. I cried in front of my son, who hasn't seen me cry very often in his life. It was awful. Walking out of that hospital and leaving him alone to have a needle stuck in his chest was one of the hardest things I have ever done. But, my boy, my strong and brave boy, watched on the monitor as the radiology technician stuck that needle in his chest and he told me later how cool it was to watch.

I spent the 6 hours that he was in the hospital sitting in my truck in the parking lot waiting for the call to tell me that I could go back in to get him. Being proactive, I took a whole bag full of work to do and books to read. But, I didn't even open the bag. I sat and cried and stared at the window of the room I knew he was in on the fourth floor. Thankfully he was able to text me and tell me that he was okay, but that's just not the same as being there. I couldn't see that he was OK. I couldn't ask questions of the nurses and doctors. I felt so helpless and like the worst mother on the planet.

On the way home he told me that the technician told him that the tumour was as big as his heart. Not much wonder he was having trouble breathing!  But, that news didn't seem to bother him at all.  All he was worried about was whether he would be able to keep working or not.

Things happened fast after that. He had a PET scan and tests on his heart – to find that he also had a moderate amount of fluid around his heart – seriously, enough already!

We finally made our way to a hematologist on July 15 and he confirmed that my boy had Stage 2A Primary Mediastinal Large B-Cell Lymphoma... in other words, a giant tumour in his chest that was essentially sitting on top of his heart. It was very close to his aorta and was putting significant pressure on his left lung. The tumour was 11.7 cm x 8.4 cm x 11.5 cm! The nightmare called 2020 just kept getting worse and worse.

The doctor said that chemotherapy would start soon and

would be followed by radiation therapy, as it was a very aggressive type of cancer. If there was any good news, it was that this type of cancer was very treatable and potentially curable.

We were given a date of July 24 to start the chemotherapy treatments, not even a full month from the day my boy drove himself to the emergency department.

Meanwhile, my *Nova Scotia Strong* clothing fundraiser was still going strong, although not as strong as in the beginning, but still keeping me busy. Here I had committed to giving away 100% of my profits to a very worthy cause, which was more money than my company had ever made since I started it, and now my son had cancer. Life, again, just didn't seem fair. I made the decision to shut the fundraiser down so that I could focus on getting my son through this nightmare, and maybe have a few dollars to pay the bills while we dealt with everything, as I didn't take a paycheque during the months of the fundraiser. I couldn't keep giving away all of my profits, my only income, with the unknown expenses of getting my son through cancer lurking in my future.

A week of feeling like I was on the craziest emotional roller coaster began on July 20, when my friend, Kim, who had been my assistant extraordinaire throughout the fundraiser, and I drove to the Canadian Red Cross offices in Dartmouth with the biggest cheque I had ever written from Countryfied Clothing. I was disappointed that we hadn't reached my goal but was thrilled to be able to donate an incredible $96,000 to the Stronger Together Nova Scotia Fund, to benefit the families and communities affected by the horrible tragedy just 3 months before. (Funny-ish story... when you are super busy and are the only employee in your business, you don't have time to do your bookkeeping, therefore you are just guessing on your actual profit margin. When I got my bookkeeping caught up weeks later, I realized that I had given away about $7,000 more than I had made... thank God for my credit line! I am grateful to have had the ability to give that extra money to such a worthy cause). I felt so proud of my little company and so grateful to be able to help in such a big way, although I knew that amount of money was not going to go far with so many people who needed help following the tragedy.

Then my feelings turned to worry as I mentally prepared for my son's first round of chemotherapy. I had been through several health issues with my children over the years. My son was born with a permanent brain injury and a hole in his heart, and we were at a medical professional of some sort almost every week for the first 6 years of his life. My oldest daughter had her lung collapse when she was 14 and was diagnosed with Multiple Sclerosis when she was 15. My youngest daughter required two day surgeries for a blocked tear duct. But none of that prepared me for the C word... Cancer.

Oddly enough, after his first round of chemotherapy, I started to relax a little. He handled the treatment so well and was being an absolute rock star. I knew that me stressing and worrying was not going to benefit anyone. I knew that I had to put my trust in his amazing medical team who knew what they were doing and how to get this dreaded disease out of my son. I knew that my son needed to see that I was strong so that he could feel strong. And I knew that I had to look after my own physical and mental health in order to get my family through this. I was the rock for everyone, but I didn't have a rock, so I had to be my own rock.

At the time of writing, my son has finished his 6 rounds of chemotherapy. He handled the whole process incredibly well. His strength and positive mindset made me more proud of him every day. However, I found myself more emotional at the end of chemotherapy than I was at the beginning. My friend had an excellent analogy... it is sort of like throwing up once you get off a rollercoaster. The end doesn't necessarily mean the end. There are still so many unknowns as we have to wait and see how well the chemotherapy worked. He will then have to have radiation therapy, which will probably take place all through the month of December. Christmas is probably going to look a lot different for my little family this year. But we will get through it together.

This year did not just affect my son and I, though. My two

daughters were deeply affected by the happenings of 2020 as well. My oldest daughter works as a Ward Clerk in an Emergency Room, a difficult place to work at any time. As I said, she also has Multiple Sclerosis, which compromises her immunity. I worried about her every day that she had to go to work and potentially be exposed to Covid-19, especially when we still didn't know much about it. I worried about her mental health as she was on the frontlines hearing the stories of the many patients coming in with their own mental health struggles due to stress that Covid-19 was adding to their life, or the many people who found it hard to cope after the shootings in April. So many people were suffering and I know how hard it is to watch that happen. But, she got through it. She is such a strong and resilient young woman that I am proud to say I raised.

And my youngest daughter also had so many changes. For over a month, we were not able to go to the barn where we board her horse because of the restrictions of Covid-19. Her horse is her therapy. The wonderful people at the barn, our barn family, are truly our family and we couldn't see them. I worried about her mental health. Not being able to have any social time other than with your mother and brother is hard for a 12-year old. To help all of us get through the tough times, we arranged Barn Family Games Night once a week, where we got together on Zoom and had so many laughs and made some memories that we will carry with us forever. However, it was a very happy day when we could all be together in the barn and have some semblance of normal in our lives.

When September rolled around, I had to make the difficult choice to keep my youngest daughter home from school, not due to Covid-19, but due to her brother's cancer treatments. I couldn't risk her even coming home with a cold while his immunity was so compromised. While all of her friends got to start their first year at the high school, she got to stay home with her mom and brother and work on her computer by herself. She has handled it well, but I know it has been hard. Like her siblings, she is so strong and resilient and she will come out of this a better person, with coping skills that will serve her well as she becomes a young adult.

2020 has been an incredible year of transformation and resilience for everyone around the world. We found ourselves working from home, homeschooling our children, navigating new rules about masks and the number of people allowed at gatherings, just to name a few of the changes. We did most of our socialization on Zoom or other video chat applications. Nothing we did was the way it used to be. We couldn't hug our friends or family. We couldn't have funerals or weddings. So many things that we took for granted were suddenly taken away by the Covid-19 restrictions. Then to have so many horrible tragedies happen in our little province tested us more than we could have ever imagined.

I have never been so proud to be a Nova Scotian. Through our hardships I saw communities pull together in ways they had never done before. I see so many vehicles with *Nova Scotia Strong* decals on the windows, people showing their pride in where we live. I see people wearing clothing promoting our beautiful province. I have seen people helping neighbours more than ever before. I see so many people supporting local businesses and making an effort to promote those businesses to their friends. I have witnessed many businesses donate their profits in such a trying time to help people in need. Even through immense tragedy and pain, we Nova Scotians, have earned our reputation of being some of the kindest and nicest people on the planet.

Today, and every day, I encourage you to see the good in the world around you. I hope you take the time to pause and breathe and see that there is good in every day, no matter how horrible that day seems. I hope you find a way to help someone who needs it. I hope you smile more and judge less.

And, through it all, I can still say that 2020 was MY year. It was my year to grow. It was my year to find strength that I didn't know I had. It was my year to help my children and complete strangers in ways I never thought possible. It was my year to reflect on what is truly important. It was my year to become a better me.

---

## About Karen Dean

Karen Dean is a resilience expert, author and speaker whose mission is to help other women find their resilience and live their best life, a purpose she lives in her own life every day. She is the proud single mother of three amazing humans who she points to as not only a source of joy but as her greatest accomplishments.

Recognized by the RBC Canadian Women Entrepreneur Awards as a Nominee in 2014, Karen has been a mentor to women in business throughout her career and was mentored herself by Arlene Dickinson of Venture Communications and CBC TV's Dragon's Den. Karen holds a Bachelor of Business Administration and a certificate in Small Business Development Training. She is also a Certified Knowledge Broker and Mastermind.com Professional.

Karen believes that helping is healing and through her business, Countryfied Clothing, she gives a portion of every sale to charitable organizations. For three months in 2020, she donated 100% of her profits from her Nova Scotia Strong clothing line to the Stronger Together Nova Scotia Fund to help the families and communities affected by the horrible mass shooting that happened in her beautiful home province of Nova Scotia, totalling $96,000.

www.KarenDeanSpeaks.com
www.CountryfiedClothing.com

# LISA DRADER-MURPHY

GRATEFUL • ALWAYS LEARNING • WOMAN OF STRENGTH
PASSIONATE • UNDEFINED

The blood rushed to my face. All of the sounds around me blurred together into a non-sensical hum. My heart began to race. The pounding in my chest was audible to me. I was shaking, weak, and I felt as though the world was spinning. I picked up my pace and by the time I had approached the door, I was almost running. Once outside, I gathered my composure and took a few deep breaths. I'd made it… this time.

It was 1994 and I had just left the grocery store in an attempt to purchase food and snacks for my 2 year old son. As a newly single parent, I had decided to seek help for the eating disorders that consumed me and had come to define me. I knew that he deserved a mother who was healthy and 100% present. And I was simply weary of fighting this battle every single day.

Grocery stores, restaurants, social gatherings – any place or event that provided food was terrifying for me. I had made the decision to begin the healing process but didn't have the tools or support yet, so my very private, white-knuckle approach was wrought with painful fits and starts.

It's hard to say exactly when my battle began – it could've been when that teacher described my face as "cherubian". Or maybe it was that time when my dad made an innocent joke about my "love handles" while we were at the swimming pool. I made mental notes and vowed to smarten up and get into shape.

My youth was filled with good food. My stay-at-home mom had fresh baking on the counter most days and our homemade meals consisted of a lot of comfort food. For as long as I can remember, mom prepared a delicious traditional meal on Sunday morning, put it in the oven, and it was ready when we returned from church.

My younger sisters and I would burst through the door of our family's bungalow and proclaim, "It smells like Sunday!" The table was set with the good dishes and main courses were placed on the table, complemented by offerings of pickles, fresh rolls, and gravy. We were usually accompanied by another family and after dad said grace, everyone dug in, and we all enjoyed the company and the hearty meal.

My first diet, at the age of 9, began immediately following my consumption of multiple helpings during one of our Sunday dinners. I felt terrible about my lack of self-control. I excused myself from the table, went to the washroom, and lifted my top in front of the mirror. I stared at my full belly and pinched my love handles so tightly that I left red marks. What was wrong with me? Why couldn't I control myself? This would become the first time of many, that I would physically punish myself for failing. I was determined to do better and exercise self-control.

By adolescence I had stretched out and was gaining the attention of boys and enjoying activities with a large group of friends. I managed it all fairly well until I was 15. I'd had a rotten day and to top it off, noticed that my jeans were getting a little bit too tight. "I can fix this", I thought to myself, "all of this, starting with this weight gain."

I kept very busy as a young person. There were school music trips and competitions, plenty of social activities with friends, vacations with extended family. All the while, I was keeping a painful secret, vacillating between dangerous bouts of starvation and binge/purge sessions. The former made me feel in control and the latter left me with incredible self-loathing. The roller coaster rendered me irritable and exhausted. At times I found it difficult to concentrate and my grades suffered. But I couldn't let anyone know. The secret I was harbouring was almost as exhausting as the illness.

My self-loathing would come and go as I paid particular attention to the scales, but it was also triggered by other disappointments in my life. If I had a disappointing grade on an assignment, or lost a loved one, or was just simply sad, my friend "ED" (eating disorder) would tap me on the shoulder, and whisper that everything would fall back into place, correctly, if I practised more control. I too often succumbed to ED's cunning lies, and the tables always inevitably turned. ED was in control. Little did I know, I had reached the top of a very slippery slope, that would continue to consume me, off and on for the next decade.

ED followed me closely, making an indelible impression during my most vulnerable times – college, marriage, my first baby, and then divorce, all by the time I was 24. Because, if I had control, everything will be ok.

I was not ok. Everything was far from ok.

I was tired of this identity that I had taken on and knew that I had to leave ED behind, for good. I fought my bad habits and read self-help books, but I was no match for this illness. Every time I tried and failed, I plummeted deeper into depression and my self-harm intensified. My final hope was in therapy.

I was terrified when I entered the office to meet Dr. Carolyn for the first time, but as was usual, I could not let her know just how imperfect my life was. I put on my fashionable armour – I wore a dress that I had made myself, my blond hair was curled and styled to perfection, my makeup was on point. Although I was finally reaching out for help with my secret, I was focused on making sure she knew that I was a polished, successful young woman in every other aspect of my life.

She saw right through my façade! Our sessions quickly evolved from casual talk about fashion and business to raw, honest dialogue. I tried to follow her guidance in between visits, but I wasn't successful. I thought, maybe if she helped me unearth the deeply hidden psychological reasons for my illness, I could peel the layers back and eventually find the truth and be healed! That wasn't working either.

I was in despair and most of the world was unaware. I was keeping busy supporting my tiny family as a freelance designer and was a budding entrepreneur. I opened a boutique called Affinities, selling heirloom baby items, home décor, and giftware that I had designed. Shortly after, I launched a direct sales division, recruiting 13 representatives from Winnipeg to Vancouver to sell the collection and it appeared to be going well. It would seem that this single parent was a business prodigy.

I had started and grown a business without any help from anyone. The media seemed enamoured with me. But I was so careful to hide my pain and reveal only perfection. The truth is, I was being consumed by ED. My mind was not being nourished. I was spending my nights feeding my disease and living on litres of diet coke and coffee to maintain my energy during the day.

My parents who lived an eight hour drive from me, came for a visit and then returned home with my son for a week long stay. Without him to care for, what little self-care I had allowed myself, also left. I immediately fell deeper into my harmful cycle until one night, I began to cry. I cried for hours. I could not stop sobbing. I had reached the end of the tunnel and there was no light. I reached out to a friend who immediately came over. She took me to the hospital, where I remained for the night.

The next morning, I had an emergency session with Dr. Carolyn. I sobbed as I told her that I could not function anymore, and that I was letting down my customers and reps due to constant errors, and that my son deserved so much more than I could give. I was broken. She let me sob and lament in my self-pity for 10 or 15 minutes.

After I'd reached the point of exhaustion and couldn't speak or cry any more, Dr. Carolyn leaned forward, looked me straight in the eye and said, "You are so smart and creative. Can you imagine what you could accomplish if you took all of this misdirected energy and focused it on something productive and fulfilling?" She gently shook her head as she spoke and her eyes filled with tears.

Something clicked. I believed her. I don't know if it was how she said it – with such sincerity, tempered with sadness and disappointment – or if it was her cumulative approach, slowly and painstakingly building my confidence despite being one of the only people in my life who knew my ugly truth. Her words and authentic delivery silenced the whispers of ED in that moment and I realized the truth. I had the power, all along. If she believed in me, knowing everything about me, I had to try to believe in myself.

I wasn't made whole overnight. Every time I experienced trauma or loss, my need for control was an open invitation to ED to distract me from feeling pain. As I practised self-nurturing and began to introduce my authentic, imperfect self to the world, my confidence improved, as did my health. And Dr. Carolyn was right! That redirected energy changed the trajectory of my life and has served me, my family, and my businesses well.

In 1997, I went on to design my own collection of women's career clothing under the label "Turbine - Power Clothes for Women". My business has grown to 4 retail stores, a manufacturing facility, a mobile boutique, and a boutique resort.

Through my business, I endeavour to empower women, in an industry that too often victimizes and intimidates women. Our runways are populated by amazing beautiful women of all sizes, ages, and colours. My painful past is no longer a secret. I try to live authentically, letting the world see the far-less-than-perfect person that I am. My hope is that the people in my life – my family, friends, team, clients – will see that vulnerability and imperfection are ok. In fact, if we hide that side too intensely, for too long, we may just implode, as I did.

It is now 2020 – the stresses of the temporary shutdown of my retail stores and all that followed, began to take a toll and reminded me of my need to be in control. I pivoted my business and kept my production staff employed, but in doing so, worked far too many hours without a day off, stopped eating healthy, and didn't make time for self-care. I worked to the point of exhaustion in the midst of fear and uncertainty.

Since that day that marked the beginning of my recovery, I've experienced many trials and tribulations. During the difficult times, ED is always waiting for the opportunity to take hold of me. This past spring, those familiar lies were whispered in my ear. I remembered Dr. Carolyn's words and refocused my energy. ED failed again and I remain… unbroken.

"… Owning our story and loving ourselves through that process is the bravest thing that we will ever do."

– DR. BRENE BROWN

## About Lisa Drader-Murphy

Canadian designer Lisa Drader-Murphy is the owner of the LDM brand, a columnist, and a public speaker. A Progress Club Women of Excellence award-winner, Drader-Murphy has also received Atlantic Business Magazine's Top 50 CEO award, two consecutive years.

After graduating, top of class, in 1990 from Form & Function Design Academy in Calgary, Lisa went on to design products for a variety of sectors, including performance clothing, ladies ready-to-wear, activewear, and children's apparel, and has contributed to styling and wardrobing for film and television productions. Lisa has held senior positions and directorships with major Canadian manufacturers of technical apparel and has consulted extensively in the design of industrial performance clothing.

Hers is a vertical operation, unique in that it houses the design, cutting, production, and retail of her collections. Lisa has grown her business to include 4 retail locations, studio, Mobile Boutique, Sea Can Fabrics (fabric store), and Willow Vale Estate (boutique resort).

Lisa has garnered coverage including CTV, CBC, Global, TNT, NY Times, USA Today, BFM France, NRJ, Canal+, Entertainment Tonight, Cosmopolitan, ELLE, Flare, and CNN. Lisa has been invited to the celebrity suites during TIFF, Golden Globes, Oscars, and Cannes Film Festival and her styles are frequently spotted on celebrities around the globe.

# Margaret Miller

WIFE • MOTHER • AUTHOR • VICTIM ADVOCATE • CABINET MINISTER

## BETTER TOGETHER

2020 has been a trying year for many. But before I tell you where we are today let me start at the beginning because there can't be a present without appreciating the past.

___

Life was good: Robert and I married in 1972 and within 2 years had our first child and started farming in Rines Creek, just outside of Shubenacadie. Soon that baby count went to 3: Monica, Jeanette and Bruce.

During those years we worked and parented as a team. Together we farmed, raised our children, and made business and personal decisions, everything. It's funny, these days there is a lot of talk about equality as a woman. In our marriage and our working lives we are equal in every way.

During this time I started a ceramic shop at home until an allergy to dust forced me to sell. In 1999, after 25 years of farming Robert and I made the difficult decision to retire. That didn't last long. A bored Robert started a logging business and I got immersed in fabric and opened a quilt shop in our new home. We found out the hard way that you can't go from working all the time to sitting home and thinking without direction.

In May of 2004, our world crumbled around our feet. Our youngest child, Bruce, was killed by a drunk driver. Bruce was a 6'3", 240 lb police officer. I thought he was invincible, indestructible and never dreamed that this could happen to us. Tragedy happens to other people. Then, as I heard the facts about impaired driving, I asked why no one was doing something about this senseless loss of life. I joined the MADD Cobequid Chapter in Truro, NS and 3 years later became the National President and spokesperson for MADD Canada. During those 3 years laws were changed across the country as I lobbied governments to make change to save lives. Sometimes it took a simple reminder and direction to change legislation. Sometimes it took a little shaming at their indifference.

Telling Bruce's story to hundreds of thousands of people saved lives, changed laws and educated teens.

And although I was the face of MADD, Robert supported me every day when he had to drive me to the airport or had to spend a week alone, because he knew it was about making sure that Bruce's life and his death mattered. We were still doing it together.

In 2012 I was asked to consider running for public office as the MLA for Hants East. I was stunned. I had worked as a lobbyist and had presented and harassed countless politicians but really, is this something I should do? Is this something I even want to do? After talking to Stephen McNeil and countless conversations with Robert, I decided to run for the seat and won. Over the next few years I became the Deputy Speaker, the Minister of Environment and Minister of Natural Resources, all roles that allowed me to serve my Province.

And as everyone who serves the Public knows, you can't

do the job without the support of family. Robert was cheering me on all the way and again, we were doing this together.

Then came 2020. The year started out wonderfully with many plans for a great year with family and friends. I had decided not to reoffer and expected an election sometime soon. It was now time for us... to enjoy our time together, our grandchildren, do some more travelling and plan the next segment of our lives.

Our doctor detected a heart issue and Robert was diagnosed with a condition that will eventually require surgery. We will handle that together.

Within a few weeks he was also diagnosed with colorectal cancer. We were shocked, scared and suddenly every day became more precious as we hung onto the hope that all would be well. Surgery followed and the prognosis is positive. I supported my husband physically and emotionally as he supported me.

Robert also needed a Cornea transplant. His vision in one eye was almost gone. The first failed but the second seems to be coming along well. I would lead him, often holding both hands when he couldn't see. I became his eyes, we worked together.

All of a sudden his kidney function dropped to levels that put him in Chronic Kidney failure. Dialysis will become part of our lives very soon. We will handle it together.

Our lives have changed in so many ways. My strong capable husband who has supported all my dreams and made our lives so much better now needed me in a way I never thought possible. That means change. Adapting, finding options that work for our new reality.

We sold our truck and RV because I found it too big to drive. But I can drive the motor home that's taken their place. We will still travel when we can and enjoy all the time left to us.

It means being strong in a different way.

It means finding humour in the little things as we navigate the health challenges facing him.

It means laughing at ourselves when we can't do everything we want and asking friends and family for help.

And giggling when you realize that when older people walk hand in hand it's not only because of love but it's holding each other up, emotionally and physically. That's us now.

It means that life changes on a dime, so love and appreciate those you love every day. We never know what tomorrow brings.

It's knowing that 2020 has been a year of change, of our evolution.

Soon, the next chapter begins and life awaits. Bring it on. We will enjoy it together.

---

## ABOUT MARGARET MILLER

Margaret's roots are in rural NS where she and her husband dairy farmed for 25 years.

Tragedy made her a victim. Her own strong will made her an advocate for other victims and finally a Cabinet Minister in the Nova Scotia Government.

# MICHELE TESSIER

---

SWEATS AND COFFEE KIND OF GIRL • DETERMINED AND RESILIENT
ENCOURAGING AND INSPIRING • HANDS-ON, VALUES-BASED LEADER
RELUCTANT ROLE MODEL

This narrative is written from the perspective of a female leader in the Royal Canadian Navy. It's more a series of rambling thoughts, really, because as I reflected on the year for this submission, so much went through my head. I didn't have direct connection to many of the challenging events we faced this year, but I certainly shared them with my military family. Most of all, I didn't feel right speaking on behalf of so many of the phenomenal women I work with, so I asked some of them to contribute a thought or two of their own. These women represent the vast wisdom, experience and fortitude of institutional leadership. Their words are imbedded in the story, and I am forever grateful for their strength, leadership, friendship and support. This is for them, and for all the amazing people I have the privilege to serve with every day.

"We grow stronger and more resilient by the challenges and adversaries we face; there is nothing we can't overcome."

— Cdr Nicole Robichaud, former Executive Officer,
HMCS FREDERICTON

On March 12th, I was enjoying some leave with my parents in Grand Bank, Newfoundland. I had been visiting with family, talking to the local Sea Cadet Corps and presenting to the students at my old high school. I was, in fact, sitting in my uncle's living room, having a cup of coffee, when the Coxswain called my cell phone. I knew I needed to take the call.

As I listened to him talk, all I could think was, "We're shutting everything down and working from home, starting tomorrow? Isn't this a little extreme?!"

Flying back to Halifax three days later, it quickly became apparent that this was just the start of something much bigger. Something unknown. Something that would change the way I would live – and lead – for the foreseeable future.

At first, working from home didn't seem like such a big deal (although I must say, I was grateful I had bought toilet paper BEFORE I went on leave, or I would have been sh!t out of luck, literally!) It was just me and the cat in my little apartment, conducting business from the dining room table. The work commute was much easier, much less stressful, and I was accomplishing a lot of other things that usually waited until the weekend (or the weekend after).

But as week three approached, I thought, "Is this it? Is this the end of the world as we know it? Am I going to die alone in this apartment with just my cat, and never see my partner, my parents, my family and friends again?" I swear to God if the radio played that "If the World Was Ending" song one more time I was going to throw it off the balcony. I don't typically suffer from anxiety, but I definitely became anxious. I watched the news WAAAY more than I ever had before. I became obsessed with the case numbers, not just in Canada, but around the world. I was fixated on the announcements – don't wear a mask; wear a mask; wash your hands; don't touch your face; stay the blazes home; get outside; don't go to the park; don't go for a drive; get some fresh air... It was exhausting, frightening, infuriating, even. I knew there were people out there dealing with anxiety, depression, addiction and other health issues. I knew so many people were out of work with nowhere to turn, and the fortunate ones still at work were at an increased vulnerability to catch a deadly virus we knew so little about. And then I put myself in the shoes of those making the decisions and guiding the way for the province. I realized that no one had ever done this before. They, like us, were learning as they were going, and hoping and praying that they were making the best decisions based on the best information available at the time. I remembered they were people, just like the rest of us, dealing with the same issues at home, and I wondered how it must have been to be in their position.

Through all of this, I was leading a ship's company as their Commanding Officer. The future HMCS MARGARET BROOKE, an Arctic and Offshore Patrol Vessel under construction at Irving Shipyards, had finally started to come together as a team, to start our collective training program – except now we couldn't go to the office. We couldn't hold meetings in the conference room or play sports together. We could only meet through phone calls and virtual platforms, and many (nearly half) of my personnel were placed on standby for OPERATION LASER, the Canadian Armed Forces ready response force in support of the government during the pandemic.

It is an interesting place to be, as the leader everyone turns to, when you don't really know the answers yourself. When you are living alone, and fearful for what could come, but you realize that you have people who are looking to you for strength, support, and encouragement in the face of uncertainty. The amazing thing about leading such great sailors is that it gives you the fortitude to press on, to endure.

By early April, my partner had arrived from half-way across the country where his Air Force training had been suspended. I was so thankful to have another human being to talk to. What this reminded me, however, is how many other people out there were still alone. We have military personnel, Regular and Reserve Force, who are posted to locations without the support of family and friends close by. The importance of checking in with our members – particularly those who were alone – became our top priority. For a group who had not yet had the opportunity to come together as a team, the support and strength of the structured divisional chain on which the military thrives was the first building block towards our unity. Supervisors checked in with their subordinates daily and brought issues to the Command Team – because despite the pandemic, the rest of the world was still spinning. Members were losing loved ones, ships were still going to sea, identification cards and security clearances were expiring, medical and dental emergencies still happened, and people were still being posted across the country. And, of course, we still had a ship under construction.

From the top of the chain, starting with my boss (the Commodore), all the way down into the various departments, communication was the key. The Coxswain and I talked daily – on the phone, by email and by text messages – consolidating the numerous (and rapidly changing) directions from the various levels of government and the CAF (Canadian Armed Forces). Every couple of days we sent out a new list of directions and held virtual "Town Halls" nearly every week. When one of our members was going through a tough time, the Coxswain and I would reach out to them individually. My friends and I got creative, having "girls' nights" on video chats across the country. I found myself making jokes and laughing again, thinking of how, in my twenties I would stand in line to get in a bar, and now in my forties I was standing in line at Walmart. I encouraged the sailors to do the same. Connect with people, take advantage of the down time, make sure you smile and laugh in the midst of all of this. We settled into a routine, and I knew I could depend on the leaders working under me to look after our people. We may not have had all the answers, but we could provide them with some direction, leadership, and a mission – stay safe, stay healthy, and be ready to move when our province needs us.

Sadly, things would not stay "stable" for long. Who could have imagined the events that the next few weeks would bring us?

There but for the grace of God...

On the morning of April 19th, feeling a little stir-crazy, my partner and I decided to take a drive. I just needed to get out of the apartment and pretend to be normal for a couple of hours. As we headed along highway 102, we noticed more and more police cars along the center median. "What is this – the COVID police?" I remarked, as we passed numerous pairs of marked cars, and several more transiting the roadway in both directions. "What is going on? Did we miss something??" The radio was playing the usual music, and we had not heard any alerts on our phones since the COVID messages we received over the Easter weekend. Everything else seeming normal, in light of the pandemic. Within a few hours we would learn of the horrors that had been unfolding since the night before, when an extremely sick man started a rampage of unimaginable atrocity. Thoughts of the innocent victims and the terrible crimes ran through my head. What if one of those police cars that had driven up behind us had been the gunman? What if he had turned on his lights and pulled us over?

Those thoughts may have initially been on my mind, but they quickly turned back to the ship's company. Were any of our people affected, harmed – or worse – in these incidents? Nova Scotia is a small, tight-knit province where you don't need six degrees of separation to make a connection. Fortunately, no one in our unit was directly affected. That didn't mean people were not getting emotional over it or struggling to process it in their own ways. Many of our sailors have young children – how do you explain to them the mounting restrictions and tragedy playing out on the television every day? Once again, all we could do as leaders was talk it through, offer support, and give them hope.

"Parents and service people alike are always looking for a plan. We live and survive on routines and schedules... March 13th, 2020 changed everything. I started my workday, not when I arrived at my office, because I was always in my office. I had to figure out postings, promotions, ship equipment acquisition, quarantine rules and workarounds, all from my dining room table. And there were no set work hours – it was sometimes an all day (and night) event. And as if that wasn't enough, I was now a fourth-grade teacher. My daughter needed my time more than ever. And she needed to be connected to her friends. And I had laundry to do. And I had to order groceries. And pick them up. And sanitize them. And not get sick. And I had to be self-aware and strong and patient because my daughter was watching.

Years of leadership and life experience helped me understand that this was temporary, and things would eventually improve. I had most certainly been through worse and persevered, and I was not alone. I decided that a lock down was something that was given to me as an opportunity to gain perspective, reflect, and make up for time I had lost with my family in service to my country. Thank goodness I had help from my husband – my hat goes off to those single parents who were managing this independently. We split chores, scheduled movie nights, went for walks, and shared quiet moments together. We set up virtual play dates. We went to repatriation ceremonies. We educated our daughter on the global pandemic, political leaders, cyber bullying, and racism. We cleaned out closets and toy boxes and donated things we no longer needed. We heard the Snowbirds fly overhead. And I held my daughter while I watched the news.

Being a leader and being a mother hold some similarities – you want to be an example, you want to ensure you protect, educate, and positively influence those in your care. You want to provide them with the tools they need to be successful. And sometimes you aren't the teacher – sometimes you are the student, growing and learning from those in your charge. Giving up on that plight is not an option, no matter what the world throws at you. Mistakes will be made in both roles but using that as a building block instead of letting it defeat you builds strength. It gives hope.

Life is not meant to be lived perfectly. There will always be loss and sadness, failure, and regret. But as long as we build from it, stand together against it, and learn from it, we can conquer even the most difficult obstacles."

- CPO2 ANGIE HANSON, F6 READINESS CHIEF,
CANADIAN FLEET ATLANTIC

With the wounds of Portapique still fresh in our minds, our people persevered. All over the city, you could see signs on the street and in windows, thanking the frontline workers and declaring "Nova Scotia Strong".

Like most people in uniform, I had been approached many times over my career by strangers thanking me for my service. I must admit it was really special to finally be able to do that for someone else. If I went to the grocery store, or the pharmacy, or saw a health care worker in the stairwell, or a postal worker making deliveries, I made a point to thank them; to remember that at a time when the vast majority of the population were hiding at home, these people were interacting with hundreds of strangers every day, consistently putting themselves at increased risk.

Once again, things seemed to be getting back to normal. And then, on April 29th, my partner saw a news headline on the internet. Canadian social media outlets had caught word of a story in the Greek press suggesting HMCS FREDERICTON's helicopter – STALKER 22 – was missing.

As a former Airborne Electronics Sensor Operator in the Sea King maritime helicopter, and now a pilot-in-training hoping to fly the new Cyclone helo, he was beside himself with worry. The military is a small family. The maritime helicopter world is a VERY small family.

When we finally received confirmation of the crash and loss of six of our personnel from the Navy and Air Force, it was devastating. Once again, I knew that in addition to being there for my partner, there would be many of my own team who knew the sailors and air crew involved in the crash, as well as the rest of our military family left behind in the ship (FREDDIE, as she is affectionately known). Once again, we passed as much information as quickly as we could to our own ship's company. And once again, we held a rather somber virtual town hall. I felt so helpless as I reached out to those friends in the Air Force community to offer anything in the form of support and condolences. I watched more news stories, saw the faces of Navy friends – like Blair, the Commanding Officer, and Nicole, the Executive Officer – and their entire team sharing their grief with the world. But not just their grief. Overshadowing this was an admirable display of strength and respect; a display of our fundamental military ethos – Duty, Loyalty, Integrity, and Courage. "This has to be the end of the bad news," I thought. We need something positive to look forward to in a time of such uncertainty.

It was not at all surprising that once again, the team rallied together in unity and support for their brothers and sisters in FREDDIE. Their ability to hold faith and keep their trust was nothing short of amazing. And once again, we helped each other stay strong.


"I was deployed in HMCS FREDERICTON from the end of January to the end of June, so though technically not in Nova Scotia during the beginning of the pandemic, I experienced some unique challenges associated with it. As a "Road to Mental Readiness" instructor (in the military), I speak a lot about Resilience and what it means. It is one thing to talk about it and quite another to practice it.

Part of being a Chief in a ship is caring for the wellbeing of the sailors in many capacities, not the least, their Mental Health. In February we watched as Covid-19 took Europe by storm and suddenly we were no longer able to go ashore in any of the amazing ports that we visited. We supported our families from across the world while schools shut down, spouses lost jobs, or found themselves having to go to work in fear. This took a profound toll on the crew. In April, we watched as our province suffered when a gunman killed 22 people, some of whom were connected to crew members and then finally, just days after holding a vigil on board for our fallen Nova Scotians, we lost our helicopter and six of our shipmates in the Ionian Sea. The loss, the tragedy was profound. The crew would go on to complete the mission after being confined to ship for 141 days.

Resilience is knowing how to react in a healthy way to the things in the world around us that we cannot make sense of. As a leader, it's knowing that you have to pick up the torch and convince everyone around you that you will care for them while you bring them forward with you. Resilience is taking the worst experience possible and refusing to remember it as a black hole in your life, but rather as the greatest challenge, and then asking yourself, "What did I learn from that experience? How has it shaped me as a leader, and how can I use these new tools to support people through future challenges?"

– CPO2 Tari Lightwood – former Operations Chief,
HMCS FREDERICTON


A few short days later, on May 3rd, Battle of the Atlantic Sunday arrived. 2020 marked the 75th anniversary, and the Navy had planned extensive commemoration events across the country. I myself was heading to St. John's, Newfoundland to lay a wreath at the gravesite of SLt Agnes Wilkie, a nursing sister and friend of Margaret Brooke, our ship's namesake. Everything was cancelled. We were ordered to stay home and watch the virtual ceremonies broadcast from ships at sea. On a brighter note, the Royal Canadian Air Force demonstration aerobatics team – the Snowbirds – were flying across the country to bring a little life and hope, and they would be flying over Halifax on that day. We encouraged our sailors to don their uniforms and stand outside their homes to watch the show, and post pictures on our ship's Facebook page to share the experience with each other. I excitedly posted the news of the air demonstration on my own social media accounts. As I wrote this reflection, I remembered an exchange I had with an older friend from central Canada. He saw my post and asked an honest question – not in disdain or disagreement, but out of curiosity. The exchange went like this:

*Friend*: "I've never understood the logical or emotional symbolism of flying military planes over urban areas or special events. What is it supposed to mean? How am I supposed to feel? It's a spectacle that's always left me puzzled."

*Me*: "I guess that's the beauty of it. Things that some of us don't understand are the very thing that stirs every emotional fiber in the rest of us. Why do people find symbolism in the playing of bagpipes, or the sounding of ships' horns, or the clanging of pots and pans... or even the firing of guns and fireworks into the air? So I offer this – with the loss in our CAF community this week, there is something important to us military folks to see our best being able to fly – not for conflict, but for the sheer joy and enjoyment, not to mention privilege of flying military aircraft in a free country. It is a demonstration of everything we are as a military – disciplined, professional, passionate, and willing to give everything for our country and fellow citizens. My other half is Air Force and a part of the Maritime Helicopter community. Every pilot, regardless of what aircraft they specialize in, trains in fixed wing aircraft doing aerobatics and close quarters manoeuvres. The Snowbirds represent the best of the best in the RCAF, something we all treasure – and for some strange reason, we find emotion, unity, and solace in these kinds of displays. It's not something I expect everyone to understand. And I harbour no ill feelings to anyone who doesn't agree with it or 'get it'. That's the beauty of what we do as a military – ensure we can all have the freedom to feel how we want to feel about things without judging others for having different feelings."

*Friend*: "Don't get me wrong – I love aircraft and the spectacle is often awesome, but I never understood what it's supposed to mean. (Your) thoughts are very helpful."

Let me tell you – from the rooftop terrace of my apartment building, the Snowbirds were a sight to behold. They were exactly the boost we needed. It was a beautiful, emotional spectacle that culminated with the formation flying RIGHT OVER OUR HEADS. I ruined my partner's video footage as I shrieked with joy, tears running down my face. All we wanted was a reprieve, a little glimmer of sunshine in the barrage of grief storms that had taken over our community, and the Snowbirds were it.

The weather was improving, case numbers in Nova Scotia were slowly on the decline, and small pieces of the economy were opening once again. Businesses worked diligently, implementing measures to keep their employees and patrons safe and breathe a little life back into the community. On the military front, we were developing a phased business resumption plan that would allow us to safely return to "normal" work.

And then, just two weeks after that beautiful air show, one of the Snowbirds crashed shortly after takeoff in Kamloops, BC. The team's Public Affairs Officer – a Nova Scotia native – would not survive. Why was the universe still doling out tragedy? Hadn't we – as a military, a province, a country – suffered enough?? It was a hard pill to swallow; a stark reminder once again, that life is uncertain, our jobs are dangerous, and you can never be completely ready for the hard times. Sometimes they just jump out of nowhere, like a Bruce Lee foot sweep or a sucker punch to the gut. You get knocked down, but you have to get right back up and fight.

"2020 has thrown some huge challenges our way, and one day we'll look back and reflect on this period and perhaps analyze how we handled it. I won't go into details about my personal struggles… We all have struggles and I don't think it's fair to compare them. What I think is important is the way in which we handle our struggles. I want to end the year feeling resilient and strong. Whether this is something the military has instilled in me, or an innate trait, I don't know. Maybe a bit of both. But I want to look back one day and feel like I came out of this experience a stronger person."

– Lt(N) Linda Coleman – Public Affairs Officer,
Maritime Forces Atlantic

These incidents are but a few of the difficult challenges we have faced as a collective community in 2020. I could go on and on. Instead I want to acknowledge what positive impacts those challenges have made. I have learned a lot this year. I have faltered at times, but I have always bounced back with renewed faith and appreciation for what I have, and for the positive things this year has brought me – because it is never all bad. As a person who spent much of the past several years in airports, I have been able to slow down for a while, to sit with my thoughts, and to reflect on what is important. I have taken the time to learn – to really learn – more about the history of intolerance, oppression and racism in my sheltered world, and to have open and frank conversations about my role moving forward. I have reconnected with friends and family in new and creative ways, and have gained a deeper appreciation for my relationships, even the difficult ones. I have learned that many of those things we get upset about are just not worth getting upset over; life is much more enjoyable if you ignore the crap and appreciate the small things. I have come to appreciate that we live in a time where we can connect in ways never before imagined. The support we need and the support we can give is literally at our fingertips whenever we want or need it. And I have learned that life is short, nothing is guaranteed, and we have to make the most of the time we have while we have it.

And perhaps one of the most beautiful things I have realized through all of this is the strength and resilience that comes from being part of a team. Our bond, forged through the challenges, failures, and victories we experience collectively, means that even when we are apart, we are still together. How we choose to play on that team and how successful that team will be is entirely up to us.

"With all that has happened this year and the impact it has had on our families, friends, colleagues, and community as a whole one can't help but feel disjointed, confused, lonely, sad, isolated, heartbroken...the list goes on. If I'm feeling these things and doing all that I can to navigate through them, then I know those around me must also be feeling similar emotions and are coping the best way they know how. Having this awareness is why I reach out to those in my community. It feels good knowing that someone is checking-in and, at the same time, I'm ensuring I'm looking after my own well-being by having meaningful conversations and interactions. What I've embraced wholeheartedly over these past few months is the idea of celebrating our accomplishments, no matter how small. This could be a promotion, finishing a project, completing a virtual working group, passing a test, making a meal, getting out of bed in the morning, reaching out and talking to a friend: they're all successes and it's important that we celebrate those in whichever way we can. This is one small way in how we can jump-back, how we can pick ourselves up from the emotions that are weighing us down and come out on the other end of it all stronger, wiser, and aware. Reach out, communicate, and celebrate!"

– CPO1 ALENA MONDELLI, FORMER COXSWAIN, HMCS TORONTO

I count myself fortunate to have exploited the leadership characteristics the Navy has instilled in and expects of me – but these traits are by no means unique to those who serve in uniform. We all have strength, resilience, and the ability to choose whether we rise or fall in the face of adversity. Several years ago I had a Commanding Officer who told me, "Anyone can be a leader when things are going good. It's how you act when things are going bad that determines your true leadership." I would suggest the same holds true for a team. We don't grow when things are easy; we grow when we are challenged.

— COMMANDER MICHELE TESSIER, COMMANDING OFFICER,
FUTURE HMCS MARGARET BROOKE

## About Commander Michele A. Tessier, OMM, CD

Cdr Michele Tessier was born and raised in Grand Bank, Newfoundland. She joined the Naval Reserve at HMCS CABOT in St. John's as a direct entry officer in 1996, on completion of a Bachelor of Arts degree at Memorial University.

Over the past 24 years, Cdr Tessier's career has included numerous sea and shore postings as well as participation in international exercises in Croatia, Germany, Norway and Africa. Her career highlights include three previous command tours including HMCS NANAIMO, HMCS GRIFFON (Thunder Bay) and Commander Coastal Forces Pacific. She relocated to Halifax, Nova Scotia in 2018, where she has assumed her position as the first Commanding Officer of the future HMCS MARGARET BROOKE, an Arctic and Offshore Patrol Vessel under construction at Irving Shipyards. She has been working in the Arctic with the Canadian Coast Guard and was a Canadian representative on the multi-national Newport Arctic Scholars Initiative.

Michele was named "Alumnus of the Month" by Memorial University's Faculty of Humanities and Social Sciences in May 2017, and was further honoured to be named one of the Women's Executive Network's

"Canada's Most Powerful Women – Top 100" for 2017. In December of 2018, she was named to the Governor General's 69th List of appointments to the Order of Military Merit.

In her spare time, she enjoys theatre, football, dance and yoga.

# MIRIAH KEARNEY

AMBITIOUS • COMPASSIONATE • GENEROUS
ADVENTUROUS • LOVING MOM AND FRIEND

On March 8, 2020 I had just returned home from the most incredible backpacking trip with my family. We had spent two glorious months in Australia, Indonesia, Malaysia, and the Philippines. We beach hopped, explored new parts of the world, read books, ate delicious food, rested, spent time together and signed off from social media. This was truly the trip of a lifetime for my two sons, ages 10 and 8, and my husband and me. People often ask what my favourite part of this time was, but honestly the whole experience was simply incredible. My husband works away so to have the time for the 4 of us to just be together without the distractions of work, technology, and life in general was blissful.

My husband worked in China, and although we were well aware of Covid-19, it seemed to mainly be contained within China itself. People were still travelling, and although the pandemic was being talked about, people still seemed utterly carefree. Although

I was on vacation from work, it was while watching beautiful sunsets on tropical beaches and during interactions with foreigners that I would get inspired about work and get excited to implement these new projects and ideas. As much as I loved our trip, I was looking forward to getting home and getting back to work. I love my job and was truly excited for our upcoming Ontario tour to showcase My Home Apparel products, and the expansion of more My Home Mercantile into more retail seasonal locations. I was returning home from two life changing months and I couldn't wait to bring my renewed sense of inspiration with me.

When we arrived in Halifax on March 8th no one at the airport, no one, even asked us where we had been or if we had any symptoms. We saw more people than usual wearing masks on our flight, but it still seemed so far away from our little corner of the world in little Nova Scotia. I wasn't worried about my companies, my staff or my husband's job. We were just excited to get home, see our puppy and get back into our routines. We arrived home rejuvenated and ready to kick off the season ahead, completely unaware of the reality we were about to face. Within 5 days, I knew the pandemic was hitting Canada and that things were getting bad. I knew I was going to have to temporarily shut my retail stores and that my staff were going to have to be laid off. I knew my husband was not going back to China anytime soon and that he would be laid off. This was truly one of the most stressful weeks of my life. The kids were now home from school, I had to tell my staff, who are like family, that they needed to stay home, and our main source of family income was virtually gone overnight.

On March 17, 2020 everything shut down for me: my stores, all online traffic stopped, all wholesale orders were cancelled, and I wasn't sure if my businesses could pull through. I still thought however, that this time would just be temporary and that within 4 weeks everything would be open and back to "normal." I was optimistic and making the best of being home with my kids, like a lot of parents, and homeschooling them. I kept in close contact and brainstormed ideas with the two staff I still had. This was a very dark time as a business owner, but I was trying to keep positive and hopeful. I was still looking for summer pop-up locations and was still planning the summer Ontario tour to showcase the clothing. But, as the days went on, it became more and more apparent that this was going to be much longer than a few weeks stuck at home.

One Friday night, April 3rd to be exact, I was facetiming with my Mom and sister and drinking wine. We were talking about the press conference earlier that day with Premier MacNeil, and I told them I was thinking of putting "Stay the Blazes HOME" on a t-shirt. They thought it was a good idea, and I decided what did I have to lose? I contacted my graphic designer friend first thing Saturday morning and by noon on April 4th, we had the shirts online and ready to go. When we launched these shirts, my whole world changed. My business is built on community, giving back, and making an impact so I knew that this particular shirt would fit into my philosophy in the same way. I decided that 100% of the profits would be donated to Shelter Nova Scotia, Feed Nova Scotia, and the QEII Covid-19 Response Fund. Now was the time to give back more than ever and it was not the time to make a profit on a Covid-19 shirt, but rather to help those in the greatest need during this time. Within 24 hours we had completely sold out of shirts and we had raised over $45,000 for local charities. The Provincial news stations had picked up on the shirts and our story was being shared all across Canada and our shirts were being sold all around the world. This truly was one of the most memorable moments in my life and was a moment full of pride, hope, and excitement.

Our shirts continued to sell out and relaunch for weeks. We created a Canadian version and continued to sell all around the world, and it was incredible to watch the huge demand grow. Within 5 days we had raised over $75,000 for charity and were continuing to sell out as quickly as we could have shirts printed. This was an extremely emotional time for me because I had truly thought my business could possibly go bankrupt, but instead we were busier than ever and raising thousands of dollars to give back to charities in need. I was able to bring most of my staff back and we were literally working around the clock to get orders out and I was working harder than I ever had. I even had to conscript my husband, sons and Mom to fold, pack, and deliver orders, and it became a whole family project.

We continue to produce the shirts and sell them, and we have so far raised a total of $120,000 for charities all across Canada including: Shelter Nova Scotia, Feed Nova Scotia, QEII Covid-19 Response Fund, Adsum House, Truro Homeless Outreach Society, Canada Help Covid-19 Response Fund, and Canada Food Banks. This was a very dark time for my small business, and this truly was the light to get me through personally and professionally. I thought to myself, "If this is how my business goes out, wouldn't this be a wonderful way to end it, by raising so much money and making an impact?"

During the Stay the Blazes HOME campaign, the devastating and senseless mass murders in Portapique and surrounding areas took place. I grew up just down the road from this area, and the news was raw, painful, and shocking. How could something like this happen in such a tight knit community in rural Nova Scotia? Like many Nova Scotians, I am still coming to terms with this horrific event that will never have any real answers. It was powerful, however, to be in Nova Scotia during this time and feel the powerful unity and strength from fellow Nova Scotians. We felt closer than ever and the home pride was surging. My Home Apparel was able to offer a piece of HOME to Canadians missing their home and to those who needed that extra piece of comfort. My business continued to surge in community support during this time, and I was able to donate $10,000 to the families affected by the tragedy due to the success the business had had over the past month.

My Home Apparel pulled itself out of the lock down period by giving back and working hard. My Home Mercantile had significant online sales as well during this time and at the end of May we were able to open our doors again. It has been an interesting and difficult 8 months, but I feel proud that I was able to pull my companies through and although I am working harder than ever, we are growing again and thriving. Our whole world has potentially changed forever because of the Global Pandemic and I am still trying to navigate these unguided roads and unpredictable paths. However, it's also been a time to reinvent new parts of the business, to focus on what's working, and to let go of what is not. In many ways, we were given a new start and it is up to us to decide what to do with it.

My husband is back to work again and is away most of the time. I am really trying hard to balance working full-time, single parenting and finding some time for myself. Life is slowly moulding into this "new normal" and I am still finding my way through it all. It's been a very tough 8 months, but there has also been tremendous joy, and it's those joyful moments I am holding onto and carrying with me as we move forward into, hopefully a better 2021.

---

## ABOUT MIRIAH KEARNEY

Miriah Kearney was born and raised in Nova Scotia. After graduating from McGill and teaching for 5 years in Calgary, Miriah always knew the East Coast was home. In 2015, Miriah founded My Home Apparel, a socially responsible company, supporting Canadian manufacturing and helping to end homelessness in Canada. Miriah currently works with homeless organizations across Canada. She also works with local not-for-profits and has been an invited guest to national conferences on ending homelessness.

In 2018, Miriah founded My Home Mercantile, the giftware division that celebrates makers and creators from all across Canada. She currently has a store in Truro and Moncton.

Miriah sits on various boards and committees in her area and believes that by working together, we build stronger communities. She has built her businesses on a similar concept of community, connection and a commitment to help those in the greatest need.

Miriah lives in Truro with her greatest inspirations: her loving husband and two beautiful boys.

www.myhomeapparel.com

# MOUNFIQ ABU

OPTIMIST • CARING • RESILIENT • RESOURCEFUL • FEARLESS

## WHAT 2020 TAUGHT ME

Writing my 2020 story was more difficult than I had imagined it would be when I decided to do it. I struggled with it a lot because remembering the trauma, losses, pain, tragedies, bad experiences, deaths, killings and protests that have happened this year alone is nerve-wracking.

I have faced many adversities in my life and have been able to overcome them with courage and fortitude. It is true as they say that "what does not kill you, makes you stronger". Therefore the fact that many of us are still standing, despite the upheavals in this gruelling year, means that we will continue to thrive as long as we never give up on ourselves by succumbing to the tough situations we face every day.

The fact is that we are more resilient and tougher than

we give ourselves credit for! We must endeavour to live our lives with a mindset to not allow our situation to determine our experiences. This is my personal mantra, and it works every time to help me overcome any challenging or difficult situation in my life. This helps me to rise above that challenge, become more grateful and learn some very hard lessons along the way.

My mission is to share the lessons I learnt but not dwell on the adversity itself. What I absolutely love is teaching, sharing and coaching other people the strategies and methods to help them turn their pain into power, maximize their potential and actualize their purpose in life so that they can lead fulfilling and successful lives personally and professionally.

I have come to accept that adversity is your greatest teacher because it forces you to become more self-aware, validate yourself, recognize your strength and eliminate your weaknesses. When you overcome adversity, you essentially discover your innate superpowers which you need to build up your potential and this gives your life purpose.

Why all this talk about adversity? Because it is a funda-mental and important part of life. It initiates change and causes people to reflect and learn. All that I have learnt in my life came from adversity. Life is not a bed of roses and if you think it is, remember that the stem of roses also has thorns.

2020 has been a year of several adversities, all coming in quick succession, one after the other it seemed, as a result, it has completely changed the trajectory of the way people used to view life; here is how it changed mine.

## MY 2020 STORY

We all know that 2020 has been a tough year. But it did not start out that way for me. 2020 was my year of promise and big aspirations!

When I moved from Nigeria to Canada with my husband

and our four children in May 2019, we all came here with big dreams and aspirations to establish our family business, an international seafood export company, in addition to starting my own Coaching Practice simultaneously.

Despite the fact that I was in a new Country and struggling to find community and assimilation, I was very optimistic about the future because, while I may be an introvert in many ways, I was also very curious and courageous in my approach to life. I try to be brave and face my fears. But you must know that I was not that way in the beginning.

Growing up in Nigeria, my beloved country, I had very low self-esteem. I was very shy, self-conscious, afraid to speak up and very timid. I was bullied in school and this affected me negatively. In 1996, a month after my 19th birthday, my beloved mother died from heart disease at only 37 years old and I realized that my younger siblings needed me as a mother figure. This made me decide to have a paradigm shift in the way I saw myself. I had to reset my mind to start leading and guiding my younger siblings to become the kind of children that our mother would be proud of, if she were alive.

The tragedy of losing my mother empowered me to develop an inner willpower and strength that I did not know I had at the time. It was actually when my beloved father died in 2006, that I had to channel the lessons from the trauma of becoming an orphan to good use.

I felt empowered to start training and coaching people when my father died. I was already a Banker but had a chance meeting with a consultant who wanted me to partner with him in his training company. I jumped at it. In fact, my very first training program in December 2006 was a few days after my mother in law died; a month after my father died. When I got a standing ovation after my very first speaking presentation, I immediately knew that this is what I was born to do!!

My life experience had built me up to lead and influence;

to develop higher effectiveness skills that I used to excel in my 13-year banking career, to launch my 14 year entrepreneurial journey as a coach/speaker/trainer and co-founder of a frozen food and export company.

These skills also helped me to be a mother figure to 3 siblings, helping me to have resilience, patience, independence, understanding, wisdom, inner strength, fortitude, mental toughness, resourcefulness, insight, strategy and time management abilities needed to be a great wife and mother to 4 children in addition to my two bonus children.

Turmoil and tragedy actually have a highly transformative effect in the mind of any person that experiences them who is willing to seek growth and development. Challenges happen in our lives to make us better and not bitter. Through challenges come an opportunity to grow in courage and fortitude in order for you to rise.

## My Canadian Immigration Journey

When I arrived in Halifax in May 2019 with my family, our first priority was to find a home and get two younger children settled in school. Our older kids already had admission into University here prior to our arrival.

My next priority was to begin setting up the business with my husband, putting proper structure in place, begin looking for suppliers and building relationships with clients. There was a lot of work to do, many processes to learn, new systems and learning how the tax system works here. With determination, proactivity, and willingness to learn, we forged ahead.

As soon as we set up an office, my third priority was to begin growing my network. I went online immediately looking for entrepreneurial events to educate and enlighten myself. I attended an entrepreneurial summit organized by Black

Business Initiative (BBI), within 2 weeks of my arrival. I met a lot of representatives of government organizations that support immigrants like myself and also support entrepreneurs. I also met a lot of entrepreneurs and even students. I was very elated to be part of the immigrant community in Nova Scotia.

I attended the Women in Business seminars and connected with several entrepreneurs in different industries. I attended several business programs with Nova Scotia Business Inc (NSBI) and meetings at Immigration Services Association of Nova Scotia (ISANS). It seemed like 2019 was moving very swiftly and in a short while it was December.

I had the opportunity to attend an awards ceremony in January 2020 organized by "My East Coast Experience" where several immigrants were being celebrated for making a difference in the province. I felicitated with all the awardees at this event and made a silent resolution to myself that I will be amongst those that will be awarded by that organization or any other similar organization by January 2021.

My coaching business was also gaining traction, I had learnt from the different events I attended on how to introduce myself in my multifaceted roles. I shared insights and experiences regularly on all my social media pages to help people build their leadership and develop a mindset reset to enable them to overcome adversity and succeed in life. I also created the ELEVATE 2020 challenge on Instagram. The new year seemed to hold a great promise for the future! The year was off to a great start; or so it seemed.

## THE TRAGEDIES OF 2020

Personally, my first sign of the devastation 2020 had in its wake was the tragic death of an outstanding athlete, father, husband, humanitarian and coach, Kobe Bryant. He died in a helicopter crash with his teenaged daughter and 9 other innocent souls while they were on their way to play a game of basketball on the 26th of January, he was only 41 years old.

His death shook me to my core, and I could not stop crying for days. A lot of people may not know this, but as a tall, skinny, and very shy teenager in the 90s who loved basketball so much, Kobe was my first super star crush (apart from Michael Jackson, of course!)

Kobe's death was a great shock to America, his fans all over the world and to the NBA. His exploits in entrepreneurship and his impact on WNBA left a huge void as well.

He was celebrated for being a great basketball player, an exceptional human being, and a phenomenal father. #girldad started trending on social media because he was a great father to his four daughters, one of whom died with him on that fateful day. The impact he made in life and especially in death showed that "it's not the length of a life that matters, but the quality of that life".

My sons idolized Kobe Bryant as a basket baller, because they also love the sport like me and actually play as well. I decided to share with them and my daughters what his greatest achievements were outside of the court. The values he held close to his heart and the way he approached his life.

As a husband, his wife shared their love story during his memorial in early February 2020. It sounded like a fairy tale, but it was all real. She shared who he was as a human and what a phenomenal father he was. His team members and colleagues shared stories about his compassion, his integrity and mastery in the game of basketball. He was a role model to millions; the world has lost a great one.

When a remarkable person dies and the whole world is talking about him, we are no longer mourning a death but celebrating a life. I learnt that how you live matters because you need to think of your legacy. How people remember you is based on how you treated them and the values you held close to your heart. It is not about material possessions but about legacy, integrity, and reputation.

## THE IMPACT OF COVID

Then came COVID in February 2020, killing thousands of people all over the world in its wake. Many great people died because of this new disease, many of them were alone because of the highly contagious nature of the illness. For their loved ones, this was very tough to grapple with. The stories of people losing their family members but not being able to see them; dropping them off in hospital and then never getting to see their bodies or being able to bury them. The world was overcome with fear and uncertainty. I actually started reducing the time I spent listening to news in April 2020 and until now I still find it hard to watch the news.

This disease is a phenomenon that is yet to be demystified and the entire world has been trying to understand its negative impact. Stay at home orders are still in force in many countries of the world. Washing your hands more frequently than before and wearing masks have become the new normal.

The first impact of this disease is that it removed the basic need of human beings to connect. People were no longer able to hug each other and had to maintain a 6 feet distance between each other. The stay at home order forced everyone into solitude and fear was reinforced in the media which affected our day-to-day lives.

Paranoia, anxiety and worry became daily emotions. We have been a bit more fortunate in Nova Scotia because we have had fewer cases and casualties than other provinces. But that has not reduced the anxiety and depression thousands of people have been experiencing for almost 8 months now.

Daily life during a pandemic is highly uncertain. Like many parents, I had to learn to homeschool my kids at the beginning of the pandemic. A simple activity like going to the store to get groceries was very tasking due to the very long queues in the grocery stores because of social distancing. The early times of this pandemic were very tough mentally, but we have been resilient, and we keep moving forward. Business was very slow and a whole lot of pivoting had to be done.

In my coaching business, I started recreating and innovating and launched a new course to give people not only hope but mindset reset skills to help them pivot, innovate, recreate and rebrand.

During this time as well, I got certified as a master coach with the Certified Coaches Federation.

The solitude for me gave way to creativity and dynamism. I also enrolled for several training programs; my intention was to make maximum use of the stay at home order.

## Nova Scotia Strong

The peace and tranquility of Nova Scotia was rudely interrupted on April 18 and April 19, 2020, when a crazed man committed multiple shootings and set fires at 16 locations in the peaceful community of Portapique in the province of Nova Scotia, my new home. It was completely devastating because 22 innocent lives were lost; their lives were cut short for no apparent reason. He also shot and injured 3 other people.

I was so scared and worried to leave the house for a few days afterwards. As a newcomer that had only just started making friends and building connections, who had moved to Canada in search of safety and security, I was rattled to my core and deeply scared.

While I summoned the courage to begin taking long walks again, my heart went out to all the families of the 22 people that died. I could not even imagine what their families would be going through.

Upon learning the names of all of the fallen heroes on

that fateful day I prayed fervently for God to give their families the fortitude to bear the incredible loss of the beloved family members and I prayed that their souls will rest in perfect peace. Amen.

According to reports, the killings were the deadliest rampage in Canadian history, exceeding the 1989 École Polytechnique massacre in Montreal, where fifteen people were killed.

"Nova Scotia Strong" started to appear at the time of the Portapique tragedy, and spread as the province lived through a series of horrible events, all coming on top of the pandemic. There was the disappearance of young Dylan Ehler from Truro. The sailors killed when their helicopter crashed in the Mediterranean. The Snowbird crash that took the life of Jenn Casey. All in the space of a few weeks.

The impact of tragedy in Portapique and the other tragedies resulting in the death of many innocent lives made the province come together with strength and purpose in the middle of a pandemic. It has made us all more resilient, empathetic and more compassionate as people.

Personally, I feel so blessed to be part of this great community. As a coach I know that tragedy, loss, and pain leave behind the gifts of resilience, patience, and empathy. We need to come together as humans, no matter our race or creed because we only have one race: the human race.

## BLACK LIVES MATTER

As a black mother, the death of young black lives in the hands of police in America this year was deeply traumatizing and impossible to accept. And I usually do not use the word "impossible". The videos of the killings on social media, though traumatic to watch, provided insight for people to be aware of how bad the situation was.

On February 22nd, 2020; Ahmaud Arbery, who was only

25 years old. On March 13th, 2020, it was Breona Taylor at only 26 years old. Then George Floyd was killed on May 25th, 2020 at only 46 years old despite crying for his mother and pleading the words "I can't breathe". On June 12th, Rayshard Brooks was killed at only 27 years old and so many other lives were taken too. Their families will never see their faces nor hear their voices again.

These deaths hit home for me as a black mother to teenage boys and girls due to the circumstances of the deaths and how they could have been avoided. Because the pandemic had made us stay at home and work from home, the solitude made me more aware and increased my empathy. As I write this my hands are shaking, and I feel a tightness on my throat.

The deaths led to protests all over the world including Canada and woke up the activist in me. It made me have difficult conversations with my kids, husband and those close to me. It made me more aware about the message of Black Lives Matter. I was particularly elated to see Canadians of every race join the worldwide protests.

These tragedies made people wake up to the need for change and the awareness was on a global scale. It made people seek enlightenment because there is a history lesson to learn from all of this as well.

I have always been a positive person, but this year has come with many tests and we are still taking the hits. It is so exhausting and emotionally draining.

#WEARETIRED

Just when I thought things couldn't get any worse, it actually did! In June 2020, a 22-year-old student in Nigeria called Uwavera Omozuwa was brutally raped and bludgeoned to death in a church where she had gone to study.

As I write this, my toes are tightening, and I am completely overcome with grief. I had to research most of these facts to write this story. I had heard the news, I had empathized and prayed when all these tragedies were happening. I had also talked to my loved ones, friends, and colleagues in Nigeria. But I didn't know all the facts of each tragic incident until I started writing this piece. It goes to show that adversities of 2020 affected everyone. No one was immune. If something did not happen to you personally, you certainly knew someone who was directly affected.

The death of the young Uwa created widespread outrage in Nigeria. It was one of several shocking cases where other young girls had been raped and killed, within the same week. A 16-year-old student Tina Ezekwe was shot dead by police in Lagos, 18-year-old woman called Jennifer was raped by five men in Kaduna in April and an 18-year-old student called Barakat Bello, was raped and murdered in her home in the south-western state of Oyo.

All these incidents led to street protests, an online petition signed by thousands and a Twitter hashtag #WeAreTired started trending as a demand for the government to take fierce action against gender-based crimes and police violence in the country.

As a Nigerian, a woman and a mother, I am grief stricken and completely shocked at this news. I am glad that the people are being made aware of the social ills of the society worldwide. The hope is that this awareness and the protests are taken seriously by those in authority so that necessary changes can be made. The only thing we can actually hold on to is hope.

Nigerians are great people; the youths are awakened and are more aware than ever! While we have many differences, tribes and political opinions we are one people and are proud to be Africans.


## DEATH TEACHES US HOW TO LIVE


Watching movies has been a great escape for many people

in 2020. Especially in the early days of the pandemic, Netflix was a great distraction from the barrage of bad news. I love movies but I am very selective about what I watch. Sometimes I love watching comedies, especially romantic comedies; but often, I need a movie to have a message, a value to teach or to influence a change. One of my all-time favourite movies was Black Panther starring the phenomenal Chadwick Boseman.

This was the one movie that had an all-black cast, the first action movie that was nominated for an Academy Award. Aside from the pride and honour I felt watching people that looked like me in a big blockbuster movie like Black Panther; it also had a great message of hope, service, heritage, honour, integrity, courage, grit, power and so much more. The women in the movie were so powerful and relevant. They were not only fierce and fabulous; they were strong, powerful, and fearless warriors. The King Tchalla was played by the real-life King Chadwick Boseman.

His grace, dignity and eloquence on and off the screen was something to behold. As he promoted the movie with his cast members and made speeches at award ceremonies, his humility was evident. His values and strong convictions were palpable, and his leadership was infectious. I was in awe of him. I really admired the man he was and learning of his death on August 29th at only 43 years old was another devastating blow of 2020 that I am still reeling from.

It is said that if only people would show appreciation to someone when they are alive as much as they do when they die. I loved Chadwick as a man of excellence. An exceptional actor who gave us really great movies. Depicting legends, dead or alive that he also admired. He was a class act on-screen and a master at his craft. I thought I loved him so much when he was alive but I loved him more after he passed because I came to know even more incredible things about him.

He was diagnosed with cancer 4 years before he passed and never made it public. He instead endured his illness in private and worked hard at his craft. He acted in 7 movies while enduring surgeries and chemotherapy. I also found out that he was a mentor to small children suffering from cancer, he was very kind and good to his co-stars and was a very good person. Just like Kobe Bryant, it seems to me that Heaven had gained angels!

Life is a gift. We should be grateful for each moment of every day. Never take anything for granted. We should be present in every situation and try to make the best of every situation that we find ourselves in.

Death is the greatest teacher because it shows us how to live. We must be mindful of how we live each day and make each moment count.

The week Chadwick died, my father in law died as well and so did my childhood friend. I can genuinely say that was the worst week of 2020.

I have made it this far in my life, not because I am any better than the thousands of people that lost their lives this year but simply because of the grace of God. I am immensely grateful to God Almighty for the gift of life. Every day, I make an intention to make each day count. Do my best and learn from my mistakes. My goal is to help thousands of people live to their fullest potential, find joy and meaning in their lives.

I believe in the value of the life of every single human on this earth. Each of us here has a purpose and it's our job to find out what it is. As you live your life, you need to seek clarity and meaning in your life, because your life has great value.

# #ENDSARS

In early October 2020, there were mass protests in Lagos, the commercial hub of my dear country, Nigeria. As reported by CNN in an article on 25th October 2020 by Stephanie Busari on CNN.com, "For nearly two weeks angry young Nigerians have taken to the streets, blocking major roads. They marched in tens of thousands chanting 'Enough is Enough' against police brutality and violence."

"The group's initial demands were for a notorious police unit known as the Special Anti-Robbery Squad, or SARS, to be shut down, but the marches have since morphed into protests campaigning for police reform and an end to bad governance in the oil-rich country…"

#endSARS was a battle outcry, the voice of the youths telling their government that they are frustrated with the way things are. This group of policemen have been brutalizing citizens for many years and too many lives have been lost as a result.

I have had my own encounter with SARS and it was not a good experience. Thousands of people joined the protests for several weeks before the government put a stop to it by bringing in soldiers and placing an indefinite curfew on the city of Lagos on the 20th of October 2020. Witnesses and the rights group Amnesty International said several people were killed and wounded when soldiers opened fire on protesters.

Reports now say that #endSARS has become a movement not just to end police brutality but to address ongoing social trauma, inadequate health care systems, inadequate educational systems, systemic corruption, poverty, insecurity, and so much more. Some of these reasons are why I moved to Canada for a better security of life, better healthcare and education for my children.

Not surprisingly, EndSARS protests in Nigeria have been compared to the Black Lives Matter fight against police brutality in the US. It has attracted massive global support with solidarity protests in the UK, US, Germany, and other parts of the world.

As the great Dr. Martin Luther King was quoted to have said: "In the final analysis, a riot is the language of the unheard…"

In conclusion, while 2020 has been a very tumultuous year; it has also been a very transformative year! It is a year that will be remembered in the pages of history in every country in the world and by every human being in the world, child, or adult. It is a year that most people will never forget. Each of us have our 2020 story; this is mine.

While this year started in a traumatic way, it has truly transformed my life exponentially. Because in every dark cloud, you can have the brightest stars. This year has been that of the greatest growth and development for me and by extension, my family. The level of maturity my children acquired this year has been tremendous.

It is also poignant to know that despite all the travails of 2020, there have been many triumphs that came with it. Looking at this whole year introspectively, I actually feel more elevated than I have ever been in every aspect of my life.

I have become more resilient, wise, resourceful, more enterprising, confident, assertive, influential and my competency as a mother, wife, and businesswoman is at its peak. So, thank you 2020 for all your lessons which have become learning points for me. 2020 has taught us so many things to make us ready for anything 2021 has to bring.

Thank you.

## About Mounfiq Abu

Mounfiq Raiyan Abu is an entrepreneur, certified coach, speaker, trainer, facilitator and writer. She is the Vice President of Ahead Fisheries Incorporated – A Canadian seafood exporting company that delivers high quality frozen fish and seafood to clients in Nigeria. As an executive and leadership coach, she has helped thousands of women to obtain clarity, realize their potential, gain confidence and overcome fears and turn their pain into power. As a result, they are able to transform into the best version of themselves.

She has 13 years banking experience, 5 years of experience as a Bank Manager, 14 years of entrepreneurial experience and counting.

She has been featured and interviewed by several newspapers and magazines in Nigeria, as well as several magazines and podcasts in Canada and the United States of America. She was also a Guest Speaker at the Network for the Empowerment of Women International Women's Day Event in Halifax.

As an entrepreneur in Halifax, she was nominated at Top Exporter of the Year 2020 in Nova Scotia by Halifax Chamber of Commerce and recognized as a dynamic entrepreneur by Immigrant Services Association of Nova Scotia (ISANS).

Her own personal growth and success came about because of some painful experiences that she endured while growing up, which culminated in the death of her dear mother when she was only 19 years old. Her death compelled Mounfiq to take the role of a mother to her 3 younger siblings and develop a growth mindset and leadership skills to help them succeed in life. She now uses her life experience, career and entrepreneurial skills to teach other people to be the best version of themselves.

She lives in Halifax, Nova Scotia with her husband and 4 children.

mounfiqraiyanabucoaching@gmail.com
mounfiq@mounfiqraiyanabu.com

www.mounfiqraiyanabu.com
www.aheadfisheries.com
www.instagram.com/raiyan_inspires

# NANCY REGAN

EMPATHETIC • FUNNY • MISCHIEVOUS • OPEN • SPIRITUAL

On March 15th, I arrived home from Florida at 1 a.m. with this phrase echoing in my head: "Beware the Ides of March". What started as a vacation, had became a rescue mission of sorts as my daughter and I brought my 84 year old mother back to Canada with us. My mom had been planning to stay 'til May, but part way through our "vacation" week there, it became apparent that getting her home to Nova Scotia was not only advisable, but necessary. We were smack dab in that pivotal week during which so many of us suddenly realized that this looming pandemic was a global catastrophe.

As quarantines go, mine was a dream. Upon our return to Nova Scotia, I drove – with my child and my parent – directly to my cottage, where we would be surrounded for the next three months by natural beauty and wildlife. Instead of being trapped in her condo in the city, my mother could walk in nature and watch deer graze right outside the door – and for that she expressed constant gratitude. Looking back now, I wonder what my initial experience of that lockdown would have been if I had been somewhere less grounded.

Because, let me be clear; I was a mess where I was.

As the news of mounting case-numbers became an underlying current beneath our days, we heard frightening stories from Italy and eventually New York City about healthcare being overwhelmed and people dying alone. Things seemed to get more chaotic every day, and to make matters worse, my two adult sons were locked down in Toronto – usually an easy flight, but now a world away.

I am prone to low-grade anxiety at the best of times. You know that saying "Don't sweat the small stuff"? Whoever coined it was probably talking to me ;)

But I've been on a path for a number of years now, moving imperfectly towards showing kindness and compassion to myself and others.

I have looked inwardly and become comfortable with what Carl Jung called my Shadow. I am self-aware enough that my heart consistently alerts me to my occasional slide into my old paradigm of panic.

Well! That first week, my heart never stopped talking to my mind…and I was able to step back and witness this "organic" coaching with fascination.

I led myself through copious breathing exercises – the same ones I teach my presentation clients when I'm leading them away from their fear of public speaking. The good news is I can personally testify to their usefulness!

As the first weeks passed, I calmed down and life in lockdown became the norm. That's when the Big Magic started.

> "A creative life is any life governed more by
> creativity than fear."
> – ELIZABETH GILBERT

I took a metaphorical page out of my favourite book – Liz Gilbert's *Big Magic: Creative Living Beyond Fear* – and started writing...

*this tornado that is Covid*
*    swirls around my head*
*hurling words and phrases*
*    demanding to be said*
*written down or spoken loud*
*    they need to be released*
*I grab my pen and paper*
*    in the hope of some relief*

*this storm is witnessed by my heart*
*    and it does what it does best*
*it knits a net of love*
*    and throw its up into the tempest*

*then gathering the mess, it pulls it in*
*    and holds it tight*
*allowing calm to settle in*
*    and bathing it in light*

*the words then start to breathe again*
*    and assemble themselves in line*
*spelling out a message*
*    as much yours as it is mine*

To say I started writing poems would be inaccurate. It was more like they started writing themselves. And in the process, they were writing me as well – or at least helping me turn a page. That led to gratitude, which circled me right back 'round to more creativity.

I was saying yes to the 'big magic' of inspiration, and it was nurturing me through this time of crisis.

I've believed for some time now (and have often said to audiences) that it's impossible to feel grateful and stressed-out at the same time. So, I amped up my gratitude and the trickle of poetry became a torrent.

Here's where I issue my patent disclaimer though, and although several friends and mentors have suggested this is a sign of my old impostor syndrome poking its way into my present, I do mean these words sincerely and humbly: my poems are simple.

They'll never win me a Pulitzer, but they give me something more valuable; peace.

Yup. They're basically therapy on the cheap.

I remember so clearly the morning it began. It was late March, but the sun was shining and after a cold stretch, the temperature had risen dramatically overnight. I was the first one up and keen to take advantage of the time alone, and my back deck beckoned to me. So I grabbed a blanket, my writing notebook, and a pen and balancing it all with a steaming cup of coffee, I went out and set myself up in a comfy wicker chair.

As I paused to take it in, I immediately became aware of the music within the silence, and a flock of unseen birds entertained me for the next 30 minutes with their melodic chatter. Here's the poem that arrived... as I arrived in the moment!

> *The language of the birds*
> *is a mystery to me*
> *but listening in the morning sun*

*my hearing helps me see*
*It unleashes me from the treadmill*
*of trying to understand*
*the opinions, facts, & figures*
*that seek an upper hand*

*This virus is unknowable*
*or at least its question - why?*
*No one can put a meaning to it*
*no matter how they try*

*"It is what is is"*
*the birds seem to sing*
*"It is -*
*and so are we*
*Feel the sorrow & joy at once*
*and that will set you free"*

Feeling the sorrow and joy at once meant accepting what was happening in the world, and simultaneously embracing the gift of this time in stillness. You see, along with the stress, I had been experiencing a type of survivor's guilt. One of my big Why's had been trying to make sense of the fact that so many people in the world were suffering in an intense way – while I was basically on vacation. Healthcare workers were risking their lives (and their families' well-being), people already living with financial hardship were on the brink of disaster, and here I was snuggled into my favourite place on Earth where I could curl up next to a fireplace while watching the waves at the beach below.

But that morning in the sun anchored me in another gift

Liz Gilbert had given me when I had interviewed her for my podcast the previous year. She had talked about accepting the good and bad in ourselves and others by having a mantra of "Yes & Yes".

When describing her support of her partner who had died of cancer, Liz posed the rhetorical question, "Was I a perfect, selfless, caring, loving, adoring caregiver... and was I also trapped in my own narcissism and pain and demands? Yes. Yes and yes. All of it."

I settled down into that sense of paradox like an overstuffed armchair. I got comfortable with it.

*Is this a prison, or a nest?*
*Don't let my mind decide*
*Pose the question to my heart*
  *"Why am I trapped inside?"*

*Is this a sentence, or a gift?*
*A death, or a rebirth?*
*The answer comes; "It's both, my love*
  *- for us, and for the Earth"*

*Like Passover & Easter*
*The duality of faith*
*calls me to embrace the Joy*
  *with tears still on my face*

*Gratitude is my best friend*
*She's wise, constant, and strong*
*She picks me up and carries me*
  *when everything goes wrong*

*Endings give me fear*
*Beginning can as well*
*The choice is mine to live this life*
*in heaven or in hell*

*So,*
*I'll eat 'til I'm full*
*Cry 'til I'm done*
*Sleep 'til I awaken*
*Rise, and greet the sun*

But then something unexpected happened and it was rooted in that concept of Yes & Yes. While I was practicing sending out loving kindness to the world, I discovered that I could also freely express my frustration and anger, and somehow ease my own sense of helplessness – through poetry.

*My neighbour the elephant*
*is in danger*
*He is cavalier*
*about a threat that impacts us*
*both*

*I am an alert mouse*
*adept at protection*
*aware of my vulnerability*
*and wise to the warnings of the*

*World*
*I fear for myself*
*but I fear for my neighbour*
*more*
*His size and strength*
*cloak him in a senile sense of*
*safety*

*He has big ears*
*but cannot hear*
*the world*
*He has thick skin*
*but a fragile heart*

*When he falls to the ground*
*The Earth will shake*

I had never been a fan of Donald Trump. His proclivity for shaming and belittling others while falsely celebrating himself rubbed against the grain of my very fabric. When he had won the 2016 election, I stayed up 'til the bitter end of the TV coverage that night. At first, I was determined to keep watching until it turned around and swung back in Hilary Clinton's favour... but as the hours ticked by and it became horrifyingly apparent that the Republicans would win the night, I couldn't take my eyes off the coverage. Like the proverbial train wreck. However, when "the Donald" took the stage to gloat, I came to a sudden and strong realization; this had to happen. I can only describe it as a knowing – an understanding and acceptance that what was unfolding was necessary to the progress of the planet. That what we were seeing laid bare was the collective representation of our societal "Shadow". And we had to face the ugliness of the racism and vitriol before we could make real progress.

All this to say, that I approached the beginning of the Trumpian age with resignation and some degree of long-range hope. But with his handling of the Pandemic – and by that, I mean mishandling – something in me snapped. I had always felt a deep purpose around supporting an underdog and standing up for those who were being treated unfairly, and now it started pouring out though my pen…

### 20/20

*they march into our hospitals*
  *soldiers in the fight*
*never signed up to risk their lives*
  *morning noon and night*

*their weapons are their stethoscopes*
  *oxygen their cure*
*but the air in there is not enough*
  *to freeze the viral blur*

*their armour is a thin disguise*
  *of masks and gloves and gown*
*the commander of their army*
  *a clueless orange clown*

*he sits atop his wartime elephant*

*waving his tattered flag*
*far from the line of battle*
　　*while bodies pile up in bags*


## #FIRE FAUCI

*hashtag fire Fauci*
*the Trumpian tweet exclaimed*
*his reputation badly bruised*
*ego erupting in pain*

*forget the expert's expertise*
*and his scientific brain*
*"He isn't nice to me"*
*the familiar fanatical refrain*

*all that matters is his votes*
*his shortsighted focus on polls*
*he'd rather a country broken by him*
*than Fauci in control*


## EASTER

*Jesus died Good Friday*
*now you're asked to do the same*

129

*by a foolish fucking narcissist*
*who can't feel others' pain*

*he's worried about the market*
*money's all he knows*
*not the beating hearts*
*and struggling lungs*
*he thinks it's all a hoax*

*while his country gasps for air*
*he'll keep licking his golden plates*
*overseeing the dismantling*
*of his dis-united states*

The anger that is all-too-evident in these poems is rooted in my compassion for others. As a textbook empath, I feel the pain of people who are suffering and powerless. And the fact that I was safe, actually amped up my sense of being called to service. The engine that was whirling in my head and heart kept churning out poetry.

Easter Monday

*Stay home*
*is a wish*
*from where she sits*
*on a bus*
*on the way*

130

*to work*

*Stay alive*
*is her goal*
*as the wheels spin*
*through a city*
*where proximity is peril*
*and pandemic preys on the poor*

*Through the window*
*the blur*
*of a world passing her by*

*Across the great divide;*
*mythical mountains -*
*Equal Opportunity & Freedom*

*She's hungry*
*She's scared*
*She's tired and defeated*
*wishing*
*she could just*
*Stay Home*

As you can see, my focus was fixed on the American landscape. My own country was taking a completely different – and much more successful – approach to the virus, and I felt deeply grateful to be Canadian. I also had a newfound appreciation for my home province of Nova Scotia. It seemed like the safest place on the planet. Until I woke up on the morning of April 19th to learn the horrific news that a crazed gunman was on the loose. Twenty-two innocent humans (and one unborn baby) lost their lives in what became the worst shooting massacre in Canadian history.

These poems truly came straight from my wounded heart:

#NovaScotiaStrong

*the ache of our hearts*

*already so sore*

*thought it couldn't get worse*

*yet now there is more*

*more Sadness*

*more Grief*

*more Pain*

*more Death*

*our hearts swell with love*

*as our lungs search for breath*

*we're all so connected*

*part of a whole*

*as we wrap virtual arms*

*'round Nova Scotia's lost souls*

Farewell from Nova Scotia

*our hearts, like our noses, are blue*
*still struggling to believe that it's true*

*mothers and daughters*
*fiddlers and fathers*
*stolen right out of our arms*

*our province is bruised*
*it's just too much to lose*
*but we're united - from city to farm*

*the friendship and love we show tourists*
*turned inward now, soothing our selves*
*let's allow tears to flow*
*and trust that we'll grow*
*strong, together*
*as we say Farewell*

Our attention really did turn inward, and amidst the profound grief that we experienced, Nova Scotia turned to love. We rallied around the victims' families, doing everything in our power to support them through their pain. The message of kindness that our Premier had been preaching throughout the pandemic, took on new meaning. But as we struggled to heal, another storm was brewing south of the border, and if would affect us all. I'll let my poems speak for themselves...

*Imagine if George was your son*
*with that knee upon his throat*
*crushing all your dreams for him*
*erasing Obama's hope*

*It's an image that should haunt us all*
*and action must ensue*
*it's not just up to "them"*
*it's up to me and you*

———

*Hey Donald, have you noticed?*
*Your country is on fire*
*'Fake news' is your battle cry*
*but you are the Liar*

*You fan the flames*
*with your idiotic tweets*
*while black & white calamity*
*is swelling in the streets*

*Protected in your garden*
*you are blind to the truth*
*Racism is your gout weed*
*It must be pulled out by the roots*

*This is a national crisis*
*Not reality TV*
*Put down the bible Donald*
*Why don't you take a knee*

*You're calling loud for force*
*when you should be preaching peace*
*Climb out of your white privilege*
*Your country cannot breathe*

———

Where are you sleeping now, Breonna?

*Your spirit is restless*
*awake and alive in the*
*hearts of millions*
*a nation's fervent love,*
*wrapped 'round you*

*If only our wishing*
*could erase that night*
*negate those bullets*
*soften the souls of that*
*swat team that*
*snuffed out your*
*LIFE*

*If only we could*
*rewind time*
*sink those slave ships*
*on their way*
*to Africa*


*What would the world be now?*


*You'd still be sleeping in your bed Breonna*
*and maybe you'd be President...*


One of my heroes – in writing & in life – was the famous author, activist and poet, Maya Angelou. She left this physical dimension in 2014, but at times during the lockdown, I felt like this wise woman I had never met was sitting with me, mentoring me from beyond the veil.

One of the things I learned from her inspiring body of work was that anger – expressed appropriately – is important and valuable. So, I guess it was natural, as I participated in my own small way in the global awakening around racism, that Maya rose up in my poetry.


An Ode to Maya Angelou


*Maya was a friend of mine*
*her poems, a guiding light*
*she spoke to me of Womanhood*
*gave permission by shining bright*

*she schooled me with her poignant words*
*to see Racism as a stain*
*she left an imprint on my soul*
*when her pen poured out her pain*

*her Caged Bird's song still echoes*
*in the chambers of my heart*
*she kept on marching forward*
*molding protests into Art*

*though life had dealt her hardships*
*she was softened by the blows*
*how she held on to her Love and Joy*
*only God really knows*

*her Black Life mattered much to me,*
*her discourses on white disguises*
*she may not be here to lead this fight*
*but her spirit surely Still Rises*

*Maya was like a mother to me*
*although I never met her*
*I'm deeply thankful for her life*
*she taught me to be better*

I wish I could wrap this up with a happy ending, but as I write this contribution to a book about resilience, I'm not convinced that I am a valid example. It's the morning of November 4th, and with last night's US election hanging in uncertainty, the turmoil – without and within – feels unprecedented. But once again, I take refuge in words.  And I bring myself back to gratitude.

*I set aside some time to write*
*but a poem hijacked my day*
*It muscled its way onto the page*
*I didn't have a say*

*Like a volcano spewing lava*
*words erupted from my soul*
*without control or direction*
*devoid of any goal*

*But they liberated my fire*
*And taught me something too*
*Reminded me freedom happens*
*When emotion's allowed to move through*

## About Nancy Regan

Nancy Regan's life has revolved around communication since she was a child. She had to learn at a young age how to use her voice effectively – just to be heard in a family of six kids!

Writing became a passion as she grew, and her love of language led to an English degree at St.FX University. However her intended path to being a teacher diverged into television due to a lucky series of circumstances. At the ripe age of twenty-two, she became the co-host of Live at 5 – a news magazine with a viewership of over a quarter million people.

Her fifteen years hosting that show afforded her extraordinary experiences – including broadcasting from such varied events as the G-7 and the Academy Awards. She also interviewed thousands of people, from individuals from all walks of life across the region, to some of the world's biggest celebrities including Oprah, Madonna, Harrison Ford, Gwyneth Paltrow, and Christopher Plummer.

Since leaving Live at 5, Nancy's career has ranged from other TV hosting roles, to professional speaking, podcasting, acting, and Communication Coaching. She has developed a passion for helping others recognize, embrace, and nurture their own light, and that has morphed into her current creative project – a book about overcoming the fear of public speaking. It is scheduled to be released by Nimbus Publishing in the Fall of 2021.

She is thrilled that her life has led her back to her love of writing, and grateful also to have the opportunity to share some of her "simple but heartfelt" poetry in this beautiful book about resilience!

You can find Nancy online by tuning in either (or both!) of her podcasts – *The Soul Booth* and *The Canadian Love Map,* or by visiting her website at nancyregan.ca

# NIKKI PORTER

EMPOWERED • DRIVEN • MINDFUL • INSPIRED • COMPASSIONATE

Like many others, I welcomed 2020 with open arms! I truly felt that it was going to be *my year*. I entered into the year lit on fire to meet my goals, make an impact and create momentum into the next five years. The year started magically; I felt supported, guided and inspired, all absolutely necessary for me to achieve my dreams as a successful entrepreneur.

I am a dreamer, a do-er and a creator and my journey is one that I feel excited every day to embark on, but it wasn't all that long ago that I felt drained, stretched too thin and out of touch with who I was and where I wanted to go.

In 2009, I became a classroom teacher with all the same vigor I bring into my entrepreneurial work today, but over time I discovered that I could not sustain that energy. After nine years of committing myself to the profession, it became very clear to me that I was not on the right path for my mental, emotional, physical and spiritual health. I'd like to share a story with you that I wrote in my book, *The Conscious Communicator*, it is one that warrants repeating and will give you great insight into my lofty 2020 goals.

In 2017, I was a new wife; my husband and I had been married for less than a year. I was the mother of a busy three-year-old, who I first left in the care of someone else to return to work at the age of four months. She was so tiny and so innocent. The nature of my career made being away from work difficult. It was then that I truly experienced deep-seated and emotionally shattering guilt for the first time.

I had felt guilt in little waves throughout life up to that point; I forgot to return my library book and found it after I had moved, I lied to my mom, I kissed a boy I was told to stay away from, I forgot to feed the dog, the list goes on. You know, those little bobbles that make you have an upset feeling in your stomach that makes you pay a little closer attention next time or not procrastinate when asked to do something important. No, this guilt was nothing like a sick feeling in my stomach as a motivator to do the right thing. It was an emotional waterfall that rushed from my head to my toes that shook me to my core.

I had been warned when I was pregnant about what some moms refer to as "mom guilt." I began experiencing this as soon as I found out I was pregnant. To hear others acknowledge it made me feel less unhinged; however, it did not make it stop. Although I had been warned and felt better knowing I was not alone, it still did not prepare me for the gravity with which the guilt would consume me. In fact, the only thing I have found that has helped it in the last three years was when I decided to start taking care of myself mentally, emotionally, and physically. You would think that focusing more on my own well-being would do the opposite, that I would feel guilty for prioritizing my needs, yet it didn't. I began to feel more in control, I was regaining energy, and I was able to see that changes needed to be made clearly.

Guilt was consuming my inner world. While on maternity

leave my substitutes, yes multiple, had a difficult time with the students on my class lists. Guilt. When I returned to work my daughter was being rocked to sleep by someone else. Guilt. My time to mark and plan lessons interrupted the little time I had with my only baby. Guilt. My husband got what was left of me at the end of a long and emotionally draining day. There was nothing left for him. Guilt. I had been so focused on my new normal I had forgotten important things, like calling my family. Guilt.

The guilt did not stop after I got into my new routine as I was reassured would happen by so many. I had a baby who slept delightfully well, bringing with it its own guilt as I spoke to new mom friends struggling night and day to get their baby to stop crying and just go to sleep. Although she was a "good" baby, she still required so much of me – every day, more and more. With every passing day, she slept a little less and needed ever-changing attention. As if that was not enough, with tears being shed in the morning and often as I laid her down to sleep at night, I also had responsibilities to help my soon-to-be husband care for our abundance of animals, what I refer to as our "fur-children."

As our home life blossomed, so did our horse business, and so did the guilt. I felt guilty for not riding my horse, not helping with chores, and without my husband quite understanding the pressure, self-induced and not, I received subtle and not so subtle jabs about my absence from the barn. He wasn't doing it to be mean or make me feel worse. I felt that he did not understand how difficult it was to be feeling like I was only able to give 25% of my effort and time to multiple things I expected myself to be able to put 100% into.

The time outside my classroom began to fill with more work and my ability to say no was non-existent. With every "yes" I felt guilty, but I knew the guilt of a "no" would be even more damaging. I felt, within my heart, that I was failing in every aspect of my life. As someone with high personal expectations, maybe due to being a teacher as well, failing was tearing me apart.

As with every career, maybe more so in public service jobs,

the expectation to give your all is put upon you by yourself and also by the ever-critical and scrutinizing public. I was not arriving to work early as I had in my first few years. I felt like I was barely able to get there at all. I was arriving on time, yet that was not good enough in my eyes. I felt as though it was not good enough in the eyes of many other teachers I passed as I felt their judging glares as I hurried by them, tea, and keys in hand. My mind was so convinced I was doing wrong that it convinced me others thought the same. I knew they had been there long before me and I was sure they felt that I was not holding up to their standard as a competent colleague. I am not sure if they were actually judging me at the time or if I was so frustrated with myself that my ego was doing a great job of making it seem like everyone else noticed I was a failure as well. If they were judging me, I do not blame them. Early on in my career I likely judged some other teacher who I thought was arriving "too late" or leaving "too early" with no regard for their life beyond the classroom. This is very common in the teaching profession, and I believe even teachers tend to make this mistake, thinking that when you become a "teacher," that is it and that title defines you entirely.

No one close to me thought I was failing. They all thought I was doing "what was best" and doing a good job at it. Or so I was told. But I felt weighted. In my mind, I was a disappointment, to the true definition of the word. I was feeling deep sadness and displeasure caused by the non-fulfillment of my hopes and expectations of myself. I was not sick or depressed, I did not suffer from post-partum, unlike so many others who suffer in denial or silence and my heart goes out to them.

I was overwhelmed with life. My personal responsibility was to make a change to allow myself to grow and offer as much to myself as I do others. To do this, I had to find the light I lost. When I began to make small changes to my daily practices, I felt my guilt shift inside me. I had moments of personal reassurance telling myself that I would get control and I would not always feel this way. One day I had the thought that I should leave teaching.

I let it sit in my mind for a while before I allowed it to escape past my lips.

Let me talk about guilt! Wow, I felt it rush over me as if to put me back in my place. How dare I walk away from something "so good". I worked hard to get to where I was, and I had a lot of help along the way from emotional and financial support from my parents to job opportunities placed practically in my lap, I had benefits, and security, and summers off. How could someone think they should leave a job where they have summers off? I allowed myself to work through these thoughts and combat them with the truth. I discovered that I already knew none of that was important.

I began slowly telling people that I was making a change and for the most part, I was met with amazing positivity. I could feel the old and inspired self I once knew surfacing at times, and as I became married to the idea of leaving my full-time teaching position, I had more of these moments and began to feel more inspired to create change.

I found myself removing the title "classroom teacher" from my shoulders like a wet blanket. I was slowly sliding it off, one shoulder at a time, and with every movement from under this blanket, I was acknowledging the weight that was being lifted. I gradually set all guilt of leaving my career as a classroom teacher aside because I discovered that it wasn't the teacher part that was unhealthy for me, it was the formal classroom part. After leaving teaching, I soon discovered my desire to teach was stronger than ever, I was just ready to teach my own curriculum in a classroom designed for growth and development, for both my students and myself, in a whole new way.

Fast forward through some major personal growth moments and massive learning curves and I was entering into 2020 with a new titles of Equestrian Mindset Coach, Podcast Host, and Author within my business, Nikki Porter Coaching. My vision was clear and my path was being paved and then came the road block that was 2020 and all it had in store for me and the rest of the world! My world was rocked in many ways, I could have chosen this year to do what was easy for me and to claim defeat and return to what I knew would offer me more stability and a more familiar pressure. I could have quit. But, instead I chose to pivot!

As the world shut down due to the spread of COVID-19, my house began to fill. Our lovely friend from Quebec was staying with us when the pandemic hit and my sister and her boyfriend needed a place to stay. Our little family of three quickly turned into a family of six, and while others were feeling isolated and alone, our house began to feel overwhelmingly full. Now, in saying this, I would not have chosen to spend our shutdown any other way or with anyone else, but we built our home without even a thought of having a child, let alone, ourselves, a child, and three other grown adults.

During my "time off", I decided to take a course or two that I felt I needed to move my very young business forward. I invested a lot of money into my education during this time and felt like I would have it all figured out by the end of quarantine. Unfortunately, when the world began to open up, I was still feeling a little shell shocked from the incredible amount of work creating a business from the ground up was taking and was clearly going to continue to take for a very long time.

In between my long hours behind my computer screen, I did have a lot of fun while most of the "non-essentials" of the world were resting. My daughter, a brilliant seven year old with not a lick of horse craze like her two parents, learned how to have fun at the barn, and we spent quality time with our animals and each other. Prior to quarantine, we would go to a local restaurant in New Brunswick, only a short fifteen minute drive for those of us in Amherst, on Tuesday nights. When the border shut down, we had to find a new routine. We cooked meals together, drank lots of wine, created evening menus and celebrated birthdays all around our own table.

When spring arrived it felt like we all had a glimmer of hope that life would soon return to normal. We weren't one hundred percent sure what the new normal would look like, and to be honest there were a few things I planned to leave behind in my new normal and a few things I had decided to adopt, inspired by our unexpected interruption to life. I could feel the weight of the winter cold lift and our spirits get lighter as the promises of April came our way. April is a special month for me. I was born in April and I always felt like it offered me a feeling of renewed life. I imagine it offered me what many get out of the beginning of a new year in January.

April started out so promising and quickly took a turn in a direction I could never even imagine possible. After April 18th and 19th of 2020, I will never feel the same about April again. I will now associate this month with unimaginable loss and hurt, but rather than allow Canada's deadliest mass shooting in modern history to destroy my favorite month of the year, I commit to it creating a month that reminds me of what I live for, one that reminds me to show up for those I love as my best self everyday because I have been taught how precious life truly is. I will not allow hate to live and grow in my heart. I commit to using the pain felt during that unspeakable time to spread more love and create an even bigger impact. In my practice I teach horse owners the importance of living and communicating consciously with an emphasis on the concept that "soft is strong". Nova Scotia showed me a beautiful example of this in real life while supporting and embracing one another during and after the shooting and it will continue to motivate my work.

Like many others, the disruption to my routine, the immense amount of unknowns, the financial pressures, the lack of answers and the fear that was flooding our media sat heavy on my heart. By early June, I found myself in an internal battle unlike one I had fought before. I have done a lot of personal healing and growth work over the last decade and I have pulled myself out of some pretty low places, but there was something about this particular time that felt different, foreign even, it was as if every cell in my body was buckling under the pressure around me, the pressure I was putting on myself and the pressure felt as the human race was learning how to navigate so many new waters.

One day, when we were finally able to social distance in small groups, I met up with two close girlfriends. I remember that day crystal clear for two reasons. First, I bought both my daughter and myself our first masks. I remember feeling strange "buying into the fear", as I heard someone else's voice play in my head as I paid for them, and even more strange putting it on my face for the first time. Funny how six months can change so much. I officially feel naked in public without my mask. The second, and more profound part of that particular day, was the absolute breakdown I experienced while feeling supported and heard by two ladies who likely felt no less a mess, but showed me the epitome of soft and strong as they listened to me.

Through sobs that started in my legs and ended at my shoulders, I let it all out. I told them I thought there might be something wrong with me. Over the last six months or so I had found it increasingly difficult to find my words, both in my head and out loud. I was having a hard time focusing, I was forgetting simple words and simple tasks, I wasn't able to articulate myself; all incredibly alarming to someone who essentially speaks for a living. There were a few other things that were weighing on me, I was less patient, I was feeling less rational, I was feeling an overall sense of pressure that was making me want to run and what did it say about me as a mindset coach if I was having these problems? I told my friends that day that I just wanted to leave everything behind. Despite my absolute gratitude I normally have for my family, my mind was telling me that it would all be better if I just packed up and started over.

Luckily, my friends showed up for me exactly as I needed them to. They let me cry it out, they met me where I was, but we all knew they weren't going to leave me there. We hiked to the bottom of a waterfall that day, my eyes red and puffy and my heart pouring out all the things it was holding inside. We sat in the woods sharing oreos, stories and feelings, knowing that coming together that day may have been a saving grace for each of us in our own ways. When it was time to head back home to our loving husbands and children, we all seemed to walk a little lighter.

With each step I took back to the truck from the bottom of that waterfall, I pictured walking away from all the pressure and overwhelm I released that day. I made a conscious choice to leave it behind rather than me leave behind all the ones I truly love, including myself. When I got back to my car after saying goodbye I felt a little more like myself than I had in a long time. I knew this was not the end to my struggle, it was just the beginning, but I was able to see my ability to work through it.

The next day, I sat in the kitchen with my husband and told him exactly what I had been feeling. I cried as he asked me what I needed from him because I still wasn't quite sure, but it turned out that what I needed was exactly what he offered me that day. He offered me his attention, his ear and his understanding, even if I knew he didn't fully understand, he was trying. That day he took all pressure off of me. He gave me everything I needed for the next few months to heal as I needed. He saw I was struggling, and when he took the time to ask me why, he discovered that I wasn't looking for him to fix anything; I just needed him to give me time.

As more restrictions lifted and the weather got warmer, we were able to head to our beach. I knew it was one of the places that would help me get back to me. I sat quietly, I listened to audiobooks, I watched the kids play, and I sat quietly some more. I watched my life for some time as if it were someone else's and saw my family and myself from another perspective. I allowed myself the time to grieve the state of the world and as I released my hurt my words slowly returned.

When I was not at the beach I continued my work at home. One habit I adopted was to love on and interact with my horse like I would have when I was a little girl. There were no horse shows due to COVID, so all pressure was off there too. When I saw him I would go to him and just say hi. My favorite time of day with him was around 10:00am every sunny morning, luckily this past summer offered us a lot of those. That was his nap time in the sun. I would grab my breakfast and run out to the pasture like I did when I was a child and eat with him. One day, as I sat next to him, eating my breakfast sandwich and drinking my tea, he laid his head on me and went fast to sleep. I wiggled underneath him and got us both comfy and I sat with him softly rubbing his cheek. He was so relaxed and trusting and I was so incredibly grateful for him and his ability to heal my heart.

As I sit and write this, it is November 11, 2020. Today is a day of Remembering. I am spending it with my husband, daughter, dog and horses. Today I am remembering those who sacrificed their lives and freedom for my own and my family's, but my remembering will not stop there. Today, and everyday, I will remember the year 2020. A year that began with hope and promise, then shook the world to its core. It knocked me off balance and left me to pick myself back up, but when I did I found myself feeling stronger and more determined than ever before.

2020 was tough, but you know what? We, the dreamers, doers and feelers of the world, are tougher and we will use the lessons learned this past year to transform us into healers, of ourselves and others. 2020 will leave behind a lot of healing to do as individuals and as a society, it will hurt and it will take time, but as we learn to let go and trust ourselves and others again, this world will be transformed by love.

Nikki Porter is an author, equestrian mindset coach, and podcast host. She teaches equestrians how to grow their mindset to shift them from feeling disconnected, frustrated, and anxious to connected, present, & confident.

Her teaching translates seamlessly into equestrians' work with their equine partners, allowing them to become the horsewoman or man they long to be while navigating their personal growth journey. Nikki is an empowerer. She uses her teaching experience from the classroom and the barn to allow her to access her client's limiting beliefs and guides them to clear up their communication with themselves and others.

www.nikkiporter.ca

# ROBIN LEGGE

---

COMPASSIONATE • ENCOURAGING CHEERLEADER • NURTURER • FUNNY

When I was approached to write a story for this book, I couldn't, for the life of me, fathom 'why'? I am a working Mom, like many, just trying to raise up a good citizen of the world, no more interesting or special than anyone else. In fact, I am also trying to help others raise up good babies, in my role as school Principal, and it is the most rewarding work I can imagine, but I digress!

Contributors to this book were asked to reflect on our experiences of 2020. While I could trace some horrific events, such as a global pandemic, the NS Mass Shooting, as well as the loss of some dear, personal loved ones, I prefer to focus on all the goodness I can as a personal mantra. For instance, quite unexpectedly, I became an aunt again; my child graduated from high school, started college and got his driver's license; and I finally fulfilled a long-time wish for a hot tub! 2020 has presented many ups, and downs, for us all.

The biggest 'up' for me was the pandemic! Yep, an UP... lots of UPS!!! We saw communities hosting distanced concerts and singalongs, realized we CAN reduce our carbon footprint easily if we decide we have the will to do so, and took stock of the fact that our most essential workers, right down to housekeeping and grocery store staff, MATTER and play valuable roles in our communities. There was an uptick in our learning of technology with Zoom meetings, online classes and virtual tours promoting a heightened awareness of our world's cultures all while sitting at home. The change in work habits, routine and being able to have time to slow down with our families, with most of us working and learning from home, was a most cherished time I hope we will one day go back to, or build into a new order; that remains to be seen. That's not to say I don't love being with my colleagues or working alongside students but, when you're the Mom of an 18 year old who prefers to be with friends, being relegated to home, together, was a treasured time I will be forever thankful for. We ate meals together, took walks with the dog, binge-watched favourite shows and movies, weren't slaves to our alarm clocks and BREATHED in just being.

I know we missed prom and graduation, but our school community came together and hosted a 'first-ever' parade to celebrate our graduates, perhaps starting a new tradition! I felt the challenges of working with horrible rural internet, but an announcement about a large infrastructure upgrade was made recently and my community is a part of it! I feared the shortages at the grocery stores, which served as a revelation as to how fragile and inter-dependent our systems are, and began to shop more mindfully, locally and, quite frankly, less often, realizing wants and needs are not the same thing. And, most importantly, I will NEVER complain about the time, the luxurious time, the pandemic gave me with my boy, soon-to-be-man, and hope you, too, can find the many silver linings the pandemic presented us with, despite its hardships. If you sit with yourself long enough, whether challenged to contribute to a book or not, and reflect on the past year, you may also find many reasons to be grateful, even under the greatest of hardships. Thanks, Covid-19!

## About Robin Legge

Robin Legge, born and raised in Halifax, and now resident of Cooks Brook, NS, is a wife, Mom of one, and 'Mom away from Mom' of 112 students at the school she is Principal of. She has spent most of her adult life pursuing higher education so she can support, mentor and lead others on their educational journeys. She enjoys spending time walking her dog, with family and friends, and singing and dancing shamelessly as often as she can!

# Sam Madore

Creative • Authentic • Empathetic • Articulate • Resilient

## Because Mum Told Me To

Five days before the provincial state of emergency was announced in Nova Scotia, my mother died.

I will never get used to saying those words and, as I write this almost eight months later, I honestly can't believe that any of it is real.

The early days of the pandemic happened in a fog. The daily reports and updates on the coronavirus happened in a fog. Contracts were cancelled, work was put on hold, I was only allowed to spend time with my husband and my dog... And, all the while, I just kind of took it all in stride. Went through the motions, I guess.

I dutifully followed along when I was told to stay home. Where would I be going right now anyway?

I happily stepped back from a couple of the events I had

been working on. How could I focus on work?

I mindlessly adjusted and retreated and followed the rules. Who has the energy for anything else?

I look back on it now and it's a lot like a bad dream. Or a movie I was watching that I kept dozing in and out of.

Sure, I felt all of the same things that everyone else was feeling in relation to what seemed like the world as we knew it shutting down. I felt all of the same shock, sadness and sympathy for those directly affected by the mass shooting in Nova Scotia in April. But all of those collective feelings – the grief, the anxiety, the uncertainty of what our "new normal" might look like – simply paled in comparison to the deep, numbing heartache I felt over losing my best friend.

My world as I knew it had ended.

You know that feeling of coming home after a long stress-ful day when your feet are aching and you're exhausted and you settle into that perfect you-shaped groove on your couch with your favourite blanket and your pup on your lap? That's what my mother was for me. That warmth. That safe place. That long exhale...

She was my comfort zone. My rock, my anchor, my cheerleader, my confidante... My ma. And, though I still feel her here with me every single day, it's hard to navigate your way through life without your compass.

Without my ma, I've taken to ugly crying in public places, wearing the same sweatpants for days on end, and answering honestly when people ask me how I am.


"I'm just okay."

"Actually, I'm having a rough week."


And guess what? I'm not sorry about it.

You may still catch me apologizing for welling up because I've had a lifetime of chronic apologizing I'm trying to shake myself of… But, in truth, I'm not sorry.

> I'm sad.
> And that's okay.
> I have good days.
> And that's okay.
> I have days when I simply can't get past my
> feelings of anger or guilt,
> and that's okay too.

I count myself very lucky to have a rolodex of thirty-nine years of happy memories with a mother and best friend that I can pull from at any moment. Some days, those memories make me smile and laugh and reminisce with my family and friends. Other days, they make me inconsolable… And it's all okay.

Memories of concerts and road trips and those hugs where her chin would tuck right into that ticklish spot on my neck. The mornings sipping tea and chatting with my ma, with Mandolin Rain on the record player in the background, are replaced with sipping alone and reflecting in awe of her incredible resilience through those toughest days. Her sense of humour right to the end. Her courage.

So, it's not that I'm not grateful for all of these memories. Believe me, I am so grateful for the time that we had… It's simply that I wanted more. And, more importantly, that she deserved more.

I have wasted a lot of my life playing it safe despite the fact that life is just too damn short. I've convinced myself that I wasn't good enough, that I didn't fit in or deserve a seat at the table. And nobody has tried to set me straight more than my mother. My whole life. Through years of depression, anxiety, irrational thinking… She always treated me with so much love, grace, kindness, patience and forgiveness. She told me over and over again how much she wished I could give myself that same grace and see myself through her eyes.

As I said one final good-bye to my mum – and in the months of grief, loneliness and self-reflection since – I think I finally do.

I finally "get" what she'd been telling me and the kindness she'd been modeling for me all those years. All those times when I was sitting off in the corner because I didn't quite "fit in" with the rest of my family. Or I didn't want to go to school because I was "sick". Or I "really should do that next play because the last one really was really good."

Though a lot of my memories from March might be blurry, this one remains very clear: In those final moments in mum's hospital room, a feeling (or a message or a wave, whatever you want to call it) washed over me... I am a warrior because of this woman. So, I am already enough.

I've said the words, I've stuck the quote on my wall and dropped it into a powerpoint presentation or two, but it finally hit me in this moment and beyond. I am enough.

I'm disappointed that it took her leaving us for me to realize what she'd been trying to teach me all along... I don't have to always be "on" to be enough. I don't have to be "the best" before I even try. Sometimes, I just have to get out the door for things to start looking up.

I know it will take time and serious discipline. I know that I'll stumble more than once (heaven knows, I already have). But, I also know that it's time for me to finally listen to my ma. And do what she has been telling me to do my whole life.

To see myself through her eyes.
To show up for myself even if I'm scared.
To do my best to break free from
all of the misguided thoughts I have about myself.
To go easy on myself when I get off track
or have to take a few steps back.
To be my true self – odd and flawed and full of
courage and grace and good days and down days

and days when all I can muster is a Murdoch Mysteries marathon and a peanut butter and cheese sandwich.

Because the reality is, pandemic or not, if I can get through the rest of my life by being kind, authentic and brave – just like my mother was – then I'll be just fine.

## About Sam Madore

Sam Madore wears many hats. A marketing and event management professional. A speaker, writer, performer, children's book author, and podcast host. A community builder and mental health advocate.

Sam thrives on collaboration, delivering consistent brand messaging, creating and executing checklists that lead to successful projects and events, and being true to herself. Her strengths are empathy, honesty and creativity and she prides herself on being a connector of people and being real.

www.thesammadore.ca

# Sarah Stewart-Clark

---

Scientist • Mother • Community Advocate • Change Maker • Inclusive and Empathetic • Unapologetically Herself

Tonight, for supper, I made peanut butter and molasses sandwiches for my family. It is all that I am capable of tonight because I can not do all the things that are expected of me. Hot tears sting my unwashed face with frustration and exhaustion because I can not do all the things. I am getting us through, each day, because that is what I must do. I put one foot ahead of the other and I get us through each day with as much love, grace, nourishment, education, personal hygiene, patience, gratitude, health and sanity as I can. More often than not, I can not do all the things.

I am living in a home I can not keep clean, which is now also my workplace, with a child needing all of his mother during a pandemic and mass shooting and I am giving him all of me that I can. I am giving my career all that I can. It is expecting impossible things from me. I can not do it all. But there is no one else to do it. So I mother, I work, I clean, I teach my

162

students, I teach grade 3 to my child, I research, I contribute to my neighborhood and community – all at the very same time. But I am doing so with hair I cut myself with a pair of children's scissors, in my pajamas that are now worn out, with a body that has not showered or exercised today because I have had no time to care for myself because I don't have time to do all the things.

Because I am human, I have days when I soar, days when I coast and this year, inevitably, there are days when I crash. I cry. I am impatient with my family. I am out. I feel as depleted as a field in a drought, after repeated crops have sucked all the life it once held. The truth is that too many roots have been pulling all of the life out of my cells, without giving back. All that I had to offer has been sucked out of me. Part of the depletion is witnessing who continues to draw from my resources until I am depleted and broken. I crack and harden in the heat of the sun, like muddy soil that lacks water and organic matter.

And in these moments, the trickles of water that save me, that restore me, that energize me and that rise with me are my girlfriends. In this year of impossible things, I found the people who include supporting me as one of their things. When each new week brings more burdens to bear, a stark truth reveals itself. Who are the people who include supporting me as one of their things? This knowledge has been my biggest blessing of 2020. It is in the honest and raw and gut wrenchingly truthful and unedited conversations with women in my life, who are also trying to do all the things, that have kept me strong in this year of impossible things. We are professional women who are working full-time. We are mothers caring for our children, and many of us are taking care of elderly parents. We are community leaders who are aware of our privilege. We are trying to use our privilege to ensure the needs of all Nova Scotians are brought to the table. The number of people depending on us to be strong seems to grow every day. We can not do all of the things.

But one of the things that we now make sure we do is

show up for raw conversations, these truthful admissions, these releases of frustration, sadness, fear, and exhaustion. That is my blessing in 2020. When all the things required of me depleted my being to the last drop, women in my life nourished me. They understood. Together we continue to rise – and I am humbled and grateful every moment for the strength of my fellow women. Their acceptance, grace, generosity, wisdom and courage to share their true self has made this year possible. We can lose everything we have in life, and continue to rise, when we have the strength of other women holding space with us, and the knowledge of what women before us have endured. It is together that we are unbreakable.

## About Sarah Stewart-Clark

Dr. Sarah Stewart-Clark is a scientist, mother, advocate and community leader. She is an Associate Professor at the Dalhousie Faculty of Agriculture where she teaches in the aquaculture program. Her research program focuses on helping oyster and mussel sectors prepare for climate change. In 2014 her work was featured on an episode of Land and Sea. Sarah has been a vocal advocate for the mental healthcare system in PEI and has operated non-profit organizations helping mothers and survivors of sexual violence. This passion led to her run for the leadership of the PC Party of PEI in 2019. She is passionate about our marine ecosystems and spends as much time as possible snorkeling along the coasts of Nova Scotia. She lives in Valley, NS with her son Rory and her husband Fraser. By openly sharing her life experiences she hopes to help other women feel less isolated.

# Tanya Priske

LEADER • COMMITTED • HARDWORK • COMPASSIONATE • SOCIABLE

## PATIENCE

2020 was *the* year.

As the executive director of the Centre for Women in Business (CWB), we had a number of special projects that would finally come to reality. Things were moving at a rapid pace and the CWB team was at the top of their game.

As the owner of a bar, we had just started a new Sunday afternoon jam session that was growing in numbers. An older crowd of music enthusiasts saw our space as the place the decompress and work off the stress of the week.

In my personal life, we were getting ready to welcome our second grandchild and excited about spending a month in the Mediterranean – my dream vacation!

When we started to hear more and more about COVID-19,

I was one of the many people that did not think it would impact our lives as dramatically as it did. I had even joked to my husband a month prior as we were renewing our business insurance that we should make sure our policy covers a pandemic. News of the Public Health Order from our Premier and Chief Medical Officer was devastating for businesses and families. I remember going into the back room, crying, and thinking "How could they do this?" Not knowing then what I know now about the leadership and tough decisions needed to get us through the first wave and to where we are now.

That same week, the Mount Saint Vincent University campus, where our offices are located, announced they were going virtual. We had just a few days to collect everything we needed to work from home. Our team began to meet virtually three times a week to stay up-to-date on information that seemed to be changing daily. We shared how we were feeling, how our own businesses were impacted, and the stories we were hearing from the woman business owners that we support.

We quickly realized from the stories we were hearing in the business community that we needed to do something, and fast. We continued to offer our advisories, programs, and events, but virtually. We increased the frequency of our virtual networking programs, pivoted our programs to address business continuity and recovery, and dedicated our communications efforts to providing helpful information and ensuring our women business owners knew they were not alone.

We recognized and reflected on our privilege to continue working while so many of our clients and members had closed their doors. This made us work even harder.

When you have a dedicated team with a strong purpose, it is remarkable what you can achieve and achieve quickly. In a short span of time, we listened to over 300 women business owners tell us their stories.

Sometimes though, no matter how hard you push forward, you can break. April was the hardest month I have ever experienced.

167

I was separated from my daughters. I couldn't be with my grandson, Van, and watch him grow. My husband was diagnosed with cancer. Friends lost their children in horrific incidents. It was too much. I literally couldn't handle any more. I cried for days. I didn't want anyone to see me like this. I wondered if this was what depression looked like.

I worried about the mental health of my team. I could see fatigue starting to set in. No matter how dedicated, passionate, or strong your team is, 2020 takes a toll. Some adjustments weren't easy. Many of my team members have businesses. We all had to adjust our homes to be places of full-time work. Many of my team have children that also needed a place for school.

Being a leader during a pandemic brought a new set of challenges for me. I still needed to provide direction, continue to implement plans, and motivate people even though I didn't know what the future held. I tried to stay ahead and informed, not only keeping up to date with what was happening in Nova Scotia but around the world.

I decided that while I couldn't change what had happened, I could fight for a different future. I still am, but with a new value top of mind.

If I had to sum up what 2020 has taught me so far, it would be patience. I learned patience and active listening with my team. Patience with my business and having to adapt to the changes that we were supporting our community to go through as well. Patience with my husband as we spent months in isolation together, not moving in different directions!

He's doing well. We spend Saturday mornings drinking coffee and re-watching movies. We listen to CBC Radio every afternoon. We go for daily walks. I am learning everything about the art of barbequing. We bought bicycles. We spend time at the beach. We slowed down. We made time for the things that our lives hadn't afforded in a long time.

No matter how chaotic, unpredictable, and challenging this year and moving forward is, I have also learned to appreciate that each day is a gift. Make each one the best one yet.

## About Tanya Priske

Tanya Priske is currently the Executive Director of the Centre for Women in Business, located on the campus of MSVU in Nova Scotia. Over the last 17 years, Tanya has dedicated her professional life to ensure the participation of women owned businesses in the entrepreneurial eco-system. As the co-owner of a small business in rural Nova Scotia, Tanya understands the unique challenges women encounter. In 2015, Diversity Canada Magazine named Tanya to its Top 10 list of Canadian women who have taken the lead in advancing the status of women, Aboriginal and first nations communities, visible minorities, persons with disabilities and the LGBTQ community. With three decades of experience in economic development, Tanya continues her mission to fill the toolbox to hone the skills of women entrepreneurs. She is also known as Nennie to her two young grandsons, Mom (or T-pain) to her twin girls, and Tan to her husband of 35 years.

# TRACY STUART

POSITIVE • ADVENTUROUS • PASSIONATE • DETERMINED • GIVING

## GOING FAR IN AN UNPREDICTABLE WORLD

What do you do when the world has been flipped upside down?

No one could have predicted just how sideways 2020 has gone down. We can all agree that this was a year for the history books, that is for sure.

As an athlete the world of uncertainty is not foreign to me. Sport has never been and never will be predictable. Just when you think a team is unbeatable, an underdog comes along and completely blows the minds of those fans who were certain that the other team would win.

Ten years ago at the World Championships in New Zealand the odds were against us 40-1. Let me put it this way: if you were going to put your money down, it wouldn't have been on us. But, guess what? The odds didn't account for the weather, the odds didn't account for years of experience, odds didn't take into account reasons why we hadn't raced earlier in the year. It simply took the results from the World Cup races that lead up to that final race of the year. On the day of the final, the wind was wild and the waves were larger than any I'd ever raced in. I wasn't the least bit phased, we trained for that moment, we anticipated every case scenario, and we were ready. We handled the conditions better than anyone else in the world; on that day we were crowned World Champions.

I tell you this story because my years on the water have helped me handle circumstances and conditions that are out of my control. My experience as an athlete taught me to focus on the things that I can control and not get weighed down by external conditions.

When we went into lockdown in mid-March I knew that we had to focus on the basic fundamentals. I have three pillars that are a MUST in my life, no matter what. To make it simple I've created the acronym FAR.

F – Fuel. Focus on whole, real food, that supports immunity and gives you energy to thrive.

A – Activity. Move your body every day, break a sweat, increase your heartrate, play.

R – Rest, recover, restore. Engage in activities that bring you joy and always get a good night's sleep.

So simple, but yet so effective. Imagine if this was your only checklist every day. This was our reality in 2020. Yes, we still needed to work, yes my girls still needed to complete their school work, yes we still needed to maintain some contact with the outside world, but that didn't consume our lives.

We spent the year in the kitchen, cooking as a family, and growing a vegetable garden that superseded our expectations.

We thoroughly enjoyed the fruits of our labour.

We really embraced outdoor activity from scavenger hunts in the woods, to walks on the beach, to family soccer games in the backyard.

We took the time to engage in our favorite things. My girls kept themselves busy with crafts, dressing up in costumes, building forts and fairy houses, and spending numerous hours playing together in their own imaginary world. I read and read and read and then journaled. I took online courses; I enjoyed learning as much as I could about gardening, bugs, and pests. My husband dove deep into professional development, teaching himself how to code. He also read and read and read feeding his mind with topics that excite him.

At the end of every day we'd go to bed with the sun, no alarms set, to ensure we'd be well rested and ready to tackle whatever challenges the next day would bring.

Despite the whirlwind around us, I'd say that I have actually enjoyed the simplicity of 2020. I have enjoyed the quiet hours in the country, tuning into the pillars that keep my family healthy and happy. The FAR philosophy that we've been living is now well established and is here to stay.

## About Tracy Stuart

Tracy Stuart holds a Masters Degree in Sport Medicine and an Undergraduate (Honors) Degree in Physical Education. She is a two-time World Champion and Olympic Bronze Medalist in rowing. She believes you should eat delicious healthy food, break a sweat every day, and do activities that rejuvenate the spirit. She loves self-care (R+F), being a mom, a wife, and living her best life!

You can follow her on:

www.instagram.com/tracylstuart
www.facebook.com/tracy.cameron
https://tstuart1.myrandf.com/ca

# THE LAST WORD

2020 has shown the true character of so many people, and it hasn't all been good. I encourage you to be kind, to support your communities and to do something every day to make yourself a better person. We can all improve in some small way each and every day.

Some tips to help build your resilience:

- Set boundaries
- Only invest your time in healthy relationships
- Get comfortable with being perfectly imperfect
- Don't let your past mistakes define you—everyone makes them and it is our strengths that power us through
- Speak kindly to yourself... always!
- Focus on what you want
- Be unapologetically you!

- Take charge of your own happiness… it is not anyone else's job to make you happy!
- Feel the feelings, then deal with the feelings

I hope you have enjoyed this book. It was truly a work of love for me.

Stay tuned for future editions of We Are Unbreakable: Raw, Real Stories of Resilience with different themes.

Let's continue to build each other up and stop trying to knock each other down!

Unapologetically,

Karen Dean

# ACKNOWLEDGEMENTS

The idea for this project was literally something I woke up with in my head one morning in mid-October of 2020 and had published by the end of November 2020. I had already written most of my chapter with the thought that it would be part of another book that I have been working on for two years. But I knew that this project needed to happen, that the world needed to hear from the amazing women of Nova Scotia, and that it needed to happen fast!

There are so many people to thank for helping turn this idea into a reality:

First, to all of the women who so willingly shared their stories, especially on such short notice, I am eternally grateful for your strength, your openness and your support of this very meaningful project. As I read your submissions, I shed lots of tears, happy tears and proud tears. You all inspire me so much.

To the amazing legal experts at McInnes Cooper, Michelle Awad, Sarah Anderson Dykema and Katie Paterno, thank you for the chats and for the advice. Your brilliant minds and willingness to go above and beyond made this project so much easier for a first-time author. I look forward to working with you all for a long time to come.

To the fabulous Rebecca Wilson of Offshoot Creative Consulting, you are the absolute best! Thank you for making this crazy idea a reality on such a short timeline. Your work is phenomenal and I can't wait to have you design more projects for me in the future.

To the goddess finder, Bernadine Umlah, of Studio Umlah, thank you for always making me look my best. You have a true gift of bringing out the inner beauty of your clients and showcasing their outer beauty in the most gorgeous photographs.

To all of my friends who have supported me in the past, but especially this year, I am forever grateful for your friendship, for you knowing when I needed a listening ear, and for your kind words and encouragement.

To my business coaches, Eleanor and Ariana, and my Incubator sisters, thank you for all of your wisdom, encouragement and ass-kicking. You ladies rock!

To my "right hand woman" through my *Nova Scotia Strong* fundraiser, Kim, may you always be that friend who has a key to my house. I love you like the sister I never had and I couldn't have made it through 2020 without you.

To my chosen "barn" family, thank you for being my outlet to unwind, for allowing me to wear my sweats without being judged, for all of the laughs and for always being a bright light in my days.

To the three incredible humans who call me "Mom", Kayleen, Hunter and Kacey, you are the lights of my life. You are the reasons I breathe. You are the reasons I continue to push myself to be a better person. You are the reasons I am so passionate about building a legacy. I hope that when I am no longer on this earth, you can look back and be proud of your mother.

Lastly, I would like to thank every single person who has ever doubted me or tried to knock me down. It is because of you that I am the strong and resilient woman that I am today. It is because of you that I am so passionate about helping and empowering others, and inspiring them to live their best life. So, thank you for the opportunity to turn all of the negatives into positives.

# OUR CAUSE

A portion of the proceeds of this work will be given to the *Nova Scotia Remembers Legacy Society* to establish a bursary program aimed at women in our communities who have overcome adversity and barriers to pursue their education and that demonstrate the qualities of resiliency and strength that are captured here in this book.

To find out more about the Legacy Society,

visit their website,

www.novascotiaremembers.ca

or find them on Facebook.

To purchase *Nova Scotia Strong* clothing, visit
www.StrongerNS.com.

# ABOUT THE AUTHOR

Karen Dean is an entrepreneur, resilience expert, author, and speaker who has lived her entire life in rural Nova Scotia. She finds immense joy in being a single mom to her three amazing children, in spending time with her cute farm animals, and in sitting on her deck looking out over the beautiful Musquodoboit River and her "little piece of paradise".

Her mission is to empower women to live their best life, no matter what the world throws at them, and to give back in huge ways through projects like this book and her Nova Scotia Strong clothing fundraiser that raised $96,000 to support the families and communities affected by the horrible mass shooting that happened in Nova Scotia in April 2020.

Karen is a firm believer in being unapologetically raw, real and honest and in sharing stories that would traditionally have been stuffed in a closet somewhere. She believes that we don't heal by keeping secrets, we heal by sharing our stories, by feeling the feelings and by letting other people know that it is perfectly okay to do the same.

"You have so many important stories to tell, and you are going to piss some people off. Tell them anyway."
– LAURA WARREN, PSYCHIC MEDIUM

You can find out more about Karen and her mission at:

www.KarenDeanSpeaks.com
www.CountryfiedClothing.com

On social media at:

@KarenDeanSpeaks
@CountryfiedClothing

To book Karen to speak at your next event and empower your audience, email:
hello@KarenDeanSpeaks.com